OC

MW01225981

2	TRON LIGHTCYCLE / *RUN*
10	TOP 5 NIGHTTIME SPECTACULARS
12	WALT DISNEY WORLD VALUE RESORTS: MORE MONEY FOR MICKEY BARS
16	FAN-FAVORITE TRADITIONS AT WDW
18	WALT'S NINE OLD ARTIFACTS YOU CAN SEE AT *DISNEY100: THE EXHIBIT*
22	THIS IS WHAT DREAMS ARE MADE OF: THE DISNEY DREAMERS ACADEMY
26	ADVICE FOR FIRST-TIMERS WITH KIDS!
28	PLANNING A TRIP TO AN INTERNATIONAL DISNEY PARK, ACCORDING TO THE EXPERTS
32	CENTERFOLD
34	HUNDRED-ACRE FEAST
39	TOP 6 *WDW MAGAZINE* MEMES
40	SECRET SNACKING
44	CAKEWORTHY: A BRAND BY AND FOR DISNEY FANS
47	THIS OR THAT
48	DISNEYBOUNDERS
50	PARANORMAL THRILLS ON SUNSET BOULEVARD
54	RECONNECT WITH THE MAGIC: DATE NIGHT AT EPCOT
57	ICE CREAM SANDWICH VS. PREMIUM BAR
58	REMEMBERING UNIVERSE OF ENERGY
61	THIS OR THAT
62	DID YOU KNOW? FAN FAVORITES AT WDW

COVER PHOTO BY JUDD HELMS

SCAN THE QR CODE OR VISIT US AT
YOUTUBE.COM/WDWMAGAZINE FOR
VIDEOS TO ENHANCE THIS ISSUE.

W D W
M A G A Z I N E

WDW Magazine (USPS 0002-2990), Issue 121 October 2023, is published monthly with 2 issues in March by CTSA LLC, c/o Freeport Press, 2127 Reiser Ave SE, New Philadelphia, OH 44663-3331. Periodicals postage paid at New Philadelphia, OH. POSTMASTER: Send address changes to Freeport Press, 2127 Reiser Ave SE, New Philadelphia, OH 44663-3331.

TRON

LIGHTCYCLE / FUN

RIDING MAGIC KINGDOM'S NEWEST THRILL COASTER

BY DANNY SHUSTER

I n 2018, my wife and I were traveling home to Canada from a personal vacation in Japan. Our flight routed through Shanghai, and we rearranged the connections to build in a roughly 48-hour layover with one goal in mind: Go to Shanghai Disney Resort. In addition to crossing another park off our Disney bucket list, going to Shanghai Disneyland meant I could ride TRON Lightcycle Power Run — fulfilling a childhood dream of *actually riding a lightcycle*.

Shanghai Disneyland was a whirlwind adventure unlike any other Disney Park we'd experienced. I *loved* the ride but did not enjoy the 13-hour flight home from Shanghai, so I was thrilled that Disney had broken ground in Magic Kingdom to build TRON Lightcycle / Run presented by Enterprise® (the American name for the ride).

INITIATE PROGRAM

Bringing this ride to Florida was a lengthy process. The Shanghai version opened in June 2016. In July 2017, Disney announced plans to bring it stateside. Construction began in February 2018 as crews cleared land in Tomorrowland behind Space Mountain. Though TRON was slated to open in 2021 as part of Walt Disney World's 50th Anniversary Celebration, COVID-19 led to construction delays, ultimately pushing the opening to spring 2023. Cast Member previews and soft openings for select guests began in February, and after nearly five years of construction, TRON made its hotly anticipated debut April 4, 2023.

DOWNLOADING BACKSTORY

You'd be forgiven if you're not fully versed in the world of *Tron*. The original film, released in 1982, had a successful, albeit modest, run at the box office, earning $33 million in the U.S. on a production budget of $17 million. Fans and critics enjoyed the film, mostly praising the — ground-breaking for the time — use of computer-generated imagery (CGI).

The story, however, is a bit confusing, especially for anyone who gets lost in techno jargon. The film found a comfortable niche and a committed fan base but failed to capture the cultural zeitgeist in the way other 1980s blockbusters like *Rambo*, *Terminator*, *Back to the Future*, and the *Indiana Jones* films did. At the 55th Academy Awards, *Tron* was nominated for both Best Costume (losing to *Gandhi*) and Best Sound (losing to *E.T. The Extra-Terrestrial*).

They haven't built a circuit that could hold you!
PHOTO BY JUDD HELMS

RIGHT: Prepare for launch. **PHOTO BY CLIFF WANG** | *BELOW: In the queue, a Siren explains the grid. Also, let's get digital, courtesy of the digitizing Shiva laser at the entrance to the indoor part of the queue.* **PHOTOS BY DANNY SHUSTER**

In 2010, *Tron: Legacy*, the sequel to the original and inspiration for the attraction, premiered. This film was a commercial success, earning $400 million at the box office globally. While more popular and mainstream than the original, the film is still regarded as more of a cult favorite.

If you have time for a double feature, it's rewarding to watch these films back-to-back. The story picks up roughly 30 years later with characters from the first installment, and it's amazing to see how far CGI progressed in the three decades between the films. Seeing the grid in the original *Tron* populated by rough polygons and basic animation morph into the stunning, lifelike digital effects of the sequel is impressive. It illustrates the vision the original film had — constrained by primitive computer graphics — and fully realizes the vision of this digital environment.

The aesthetic of *Tron: Legacy* is what the attraction is modeled on; Disney Imagineers have done an impeccable job of translating the digital grid for Magic Kingdom. *Tron: Legacy* also has an incredible original score by Daft Punk (who have a cameo in the film around the 70-minute mark); listen for this music, including the breakout track "Derezzed," on the ride.

PROGRAM ERROR
I love TRON as a ride: Lightcycles are *awesome*, and the idea of transporting into the digital world excites me. I'm a franchise fan, and this ride makes my geeky heart happy. But honestly, you don't need to watch either film or the animated show (Disney made an animated series that fills in the timeline between the two films) or play any of the video games to appreciate the attraction.

The most basic level of backstory you need to understand is that "The Grid" is the virtual world, inside the computer, where much of the films take place. You are a User (a human using a computer) who has been digitized into the grid. The grid is populated by programs (literal computer programs) that, until the events of the first film, believed Users (humans) were just a myth. There are good and bad programs inside the grid; some are actively working against the Users, and others like Tron — a security program from the first film — "fight for the User" (Tron's rallying cry).

There are a number of gladiator-style games in the grid where programs compete under the threat of "derezzing" (slang for "deresolution," or being deleted). The lightcycle race is one such game — arguably the coolest and most visually interesting one. As a rider aboard TRON, you and your fellow park guests are on Team Blue in a high-stakes race against some rogue programs (Team Orange).

A female narrator (a "Siren") will explain the necessary bits of lore to you during the queue. Even if you don't register the nuances of the grid, you'll at least understand the concept of a race — at the end of the day, TRON is a high-speed race, and you want to win it.

For franchise fans, entering the queue is delightful. For instance, you'll spot a giant ENCOM SHV 20905 digitizing laser (aka the Shiva laser) positioned above you as you enter the indoor portion of the queue; this is the technology from the films that digitizes humans to enter the grid. I squealed in nerdy delight seeing the laser, and, for the uninitiated, it's still a cool, futuristic bit of set dressing. Once you step inside the ride building, you'll

PREVIOUS: TRON has changed the face of Tomorrowland. **PHOTO BY LAURIE SAPP**

READ THE MANUAL
Currently, you'll either need to secure a spot in the Virtual Queue or purchase an Individual Lightning Lane to ride TRON. At the time of publication, there is no standby queue option. The Virtual Queue opens twice a day for park guests (7 a.m. and 1 p.m.) with a third chance at 6 p.m. for guests at eligible Disney Resort Hotels on select extended evening hour nights at Magic Kingdom. Pricing is demand-based for the Individual Lightning Lanes and fluctuates daily.

WANT TO KNOW MORE ABOUT LIGHTNING LANES? YOUR WISH IS OUR COMMAND!

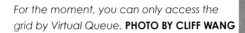

For the moment, you can only access the grid by Virtual Queue. **PHOTO BY CLIFF WANG**

see how intricately Disney Imagineers have brought the aesthetic of *Tron: Legacy* to life. It really feels like you've left Magic Kingdom behind and transported into the grid. (It doesn't hurt that you can bop along to the infectious sounds of Daft Punk's *Tron: Legacy* score as you move through the queue.)

UPDATING TOMORROWLAND
TRON has literally changed the face of Tomorrowland. It's impossible to miss the swooping canopy that covers the outdoor portion of the ride, and once the sun sets, TRON illuminates the night sky with a mesmerizing light display.

During our preview of TRON, we spoke with Randy Fox, Principal Show Lighting Designer from Walt Disney Imagineering; Fox was part of the team who brought the iconic TRON lights to life.

"The canopy is one of my favorite parts of the entire experience," Fox said. "There are over 1,200 lighting fixtures in the canopy above your head … The canopy reacts to the lightcycle as it travels along the upload conduit. It's also in synchronization with the music you hear as you come up and helps drive the emotion between Team Orange and Team Blue and the battle that's going on."

While the canopy looks great during the day, there's no denying just how remarkable the structure is at night. It's mesmerizing to see the pulsating colors, the unique reflections, and the way the canopy reacts to the lightcycles that whizz past.

PREPARE TO BE DIGITIZED
TRON is unique among Disney thrill rides, with a couple of quirks to the boarding and queue. The ride vehicle resembles a futuristic motorcycle; you straddle the vehicle and lean forward to get into riding position. If you're concerned about fitting into the vehicle, you can do a test fit with the demo units out front. I find them similar to the ride vehicles for Flight of Passage; if you can fit in one, you'll probably fit in the other. If you don't fit in the standard lightcycle car or if you can't ride in the straddling position, you can queue up for more traditional bucket seats in the back row that are more accommodating. Guests in wheelchairs or ECVs will need to transfer to ride.

Randy Fox lights up TRON — literally! **PHOTO BY DANNY SHUSTER**

"THERE ARE OVER 1,200 LIGHTING FIXTURES IN THE CANOPY ABOVE YOUR HEAD."

Don't forget to look up — the canopy lights react as riders fly by.
PHOTO BY JUDD HELMS

TRON comes alive after dark. **PHOTO BY JUDD HELMS**

Coaster junkies, thrill-seekers, and Tron fans alike will all delight in TRON Lightcycle / Run.

PHOTOS BY JUDD HELMS

Then there are the lockers. TRON goes fast, like *really fast*. Combine the high speed and the unique ride vehicle design, and there's no way you can hold onto personal items or keep them in your pockets. There's a small compartment on the ride vehicle itself, but it's only large enough for your phone or a pair of sunglasses. Anything larger must be stored in the provided lockers.

Don't worry: You won't miss them. As you approach the boarding zone of the ride, you'll see hundreds of lockers. Head to any locker that's illuminated and tap your MagicBand or physical park ticket to unlock. Stow your gear inside and then continue on to the final stage of the queue. These innovative lockers are double-sided, so as you exit the ride, you can unlock your locker from the other side, grab your gear, and go. The whole system is straightforward and works

Everything but your phone and glasses won't fit on the ride, but don't worry — Disney has an ingenious locker system. **PHOTO BY LAURIE SAPP**

smoothly, but Cast Members are on hand if you're having difficulties. Disney also offers handy touchscreens to which you can tap your MagicBand if you've forgotten your locker number.

Once you're settled into your lightcycle, prepare for launch. TRON rockets out of the starting gate and quickly hits a top speed of 59 mph, putting it just behind *Guardians of the Galaxy*: Cosmic Rewind, which is the fastest coaster at Walt Disney World. (Test Track is faster but is a thrill ride, not a coaster.)

After launch, your lightcycle races through huge banking turns and tight spirals as you fly over the outdoor walkway in Tomorrowland and back into the show building. Sitting in the front car is exhilarating, and you get the full effect of the wind whipping your face. But trust me, you'll feel the thrills and speed no matter which position you're in. As you reenter the show building, you'll be immersed within massive screens, and Team Orange, your competition, races into view. The ride twists and turns through a series of checkpoint gates and — spoiler warning — Team Blue always manages to squeak out the win. The race ends with Team Orange getting derezzed in the background as you coast to victory.

TRON has quickly become one of my favorite thrill rides at WDW. I have no issues fitting in the ride vehicle and actually find it more comfortable than the shoulder restraints of coasters like Expedition Everest and Rock 'n' Roller Coaster. And as someone who struggles on Cosmic Rewind, I don't find TRON to be nauseating. I'm particularly susceptible to nausea with twists and spins, but the wide banking turns

on TRON are much easier to handle. In fact, I was able to ride TRON back-to-back during our media preview with no ill effects.

PHOTO FINISH
Don't forget about Disney PhotoPass. TRON is the 15th attraction at WDW to offer on-ride capture, including both still images and video.

"No matter what side of the train you're on, you're going to be front and center of your photo," Jeff Harmon, Manager, Disney Photo Imaging at The Walt Disney Company, told us during the media preview.

The PhotoPass magic extends outside the attraction with special TRON-themed Magic Shots, including a physical identity disc prop guests can pose with and a special Magic Shot designed to mimic the look of the original *Tron* film poster. These shots are available day and night, but the effect really shines after dark.

END OF LINE
TRON is a great addition to Tomorrowland; it brings huge visual interest and fresh life into the landscape and offers guests an exhilarating ride experience. Fans of the franchise can revel in the details while the uninitiated can simply be swept up in the high-concept visual appeal of the ride. For coaster junkies and thrill-seekers, the ride delivers, starting strong with a signature launch experience and keeping the intensity high until the finish line. 🐭

 WELCOME, USER. ENTER THE GRID WITH US ON YOUTUBE.

No matter where you sit on the ride, your PhotoPass photo (LEFT) puts you front and center, but for Magic Shots (RIGHT), aim to ride after dark.
DISNEY PHOTOPASS

TOP 5
Nighttime Spectaculars

BY MELISSA RICHESON

When the sun sets at Walt Disney World, guests get treated to a crescendo of magic in the form of nighttime spectaculars. Let's take a look at the top five ways Disney has capped off the night with a bang over the years.

5

Star Wars: **A Galactic Spectacular**

Star Wars: A Galactic Spectacular was an out-of-this-world nighttime spectacular that ran in the late 2010s at Disney's Hollywood Studios. The show included fireworks, lasers, pyrotechnics, and saga-related projections on Grauman's Chinese Theatre and surrounding buildings. With flawless coordination of the musical score and all the special effects, *Star Wars*: A Galactic Spectacular created the illusion of being in the middle of AT-AT and starfighter battles, with lasers *pew-pewing* all around.

4

Rivers of Light

Animal Kingdom isn't known for over-the-top nighttime shows. After all, fireworks would stress the park's residents. However, Rivers of Light, shown in two different versions from 2017 to 2020, proved a perfect, peaceful presentation with a serene fusion of water screens, lighting, music, and live performers. Twinkling trees created a magical backdrop for a display of floating fountains and beautiful boats, all meant to create a sense of oneness with nature. While the effects were impressive, the show held a different, more understated tone than other Disney nighttime spectaculars.

3

Fantasmic!

When Disney dedicates an entire amphitheater to one show, you know it has to be good! Since it opened in 1998, Fantasmic! has been a must-see for most Hollywood Studios guests. And it's easy to see why. Mickey's dream turns into a nightmare when classic Disney Villains hijack the storyline. But with the help of some great heroes and a good dose of imagination, Mickey reclaims his dream. Imagineers updated the pyrotechnics, audio, and characters in this 29-minute show in fall 2022, making it worthy of a spot on every Disney World itinerary after all these years.

2

IllumiNations

Many EPCOT fans mourned the ending of IllumiNations in 2019. The show debuted in 1988 and, like other nighttime spectaculars, went through several iterations over the years. Decades of Walt Disney World guests hold fond memories of IllumiNations in one form or another. The most recent version, IllumiNations: Reflections of Earth, is likely the most familiar. The iconic floating globe captured attention from every angle around the lagoon, while large torches and illuminated buildings around World Showcase created a sense of wonder. Accompanied by gorgeous music and stunning fireworks, the show spoke to the connectedness of humanity throughout time.

1

Happily Ever After

When we polled our fans about their favorite nighttime spectacular, Magic Kingdom's Happily Ever After won by a wide margin. Gathering along Main Street to watch the magical projections and impressive fireworks makes you feel both nostalgic and fully alive at the same time. As guests view a series of powerful moments from Disney stories, it's not uncommon to shed a few (happy) tears. Plus, a soaring score with both original and familiar musical numbers tugs at heartstrings and pulls guests into the experience. Happily Ever After lives up to its name as the perfect ending to every fairy-tale Disney day — the makings of a truly spectacular night!

PREVIOUS: From 2017-2020, Rivers of Light offered Animal Kingdom guests a serene way to wind down at the end of the day.
PHOTO BY CLIFF WANG

WALT DISNEY WORLD VALUE RESORTS

MORE MONEY FOR MICKEY BARS

BY TIMOTHY MOORE

Pop Century holds a special place in my heart: If my grandparents weren't pitching a tent at The Campsites at Disney's Fort Wilderness Resort during their nearly 50 years of visiting the Most Magical Place on Earth, they were staying at Pop Century, saving a buck to fund a longer stay. It's one of their favorite spots at Walt Disney World.

That's what I love about staying at *any* Value Resort at Disney. With the money I save over a Moderate or Deluxe Resort, I can often stay longer, dine more luxuriously, and afford extras — such as tours, Genie+, and more drinks around the world — that I would otherwise forego.

That's not to say there isn't merit in a Moderate or Deluxe stay. There's something special about strolling the quiet streets of either Port Orleans Resort, lounging by the Lava Pool at the Poly, or stepping out of your room to be greeted by the massive Wilderness Lodge Christmas tree. But if you're hoping to fund an extra-long stay at Disney World, want to pay for some of the more unique experiences (check out Drawn to Life at Disney Springs!), or simply enjoy large-scale character theming, a Value Resort may be the right call.

But how do you know which one is right for you?

DISNEY'S POP CENTURY RESORT
Best for Skyliner Access

Our readers have spoken: Pop Century is the preferred Value Resort. Its nostalgic theming likely evokes memories for parents and grandparents while little ones will simply love the hotel's three pools (the Hippy Dippy Pool is the largest and most centrally located, but the Bowling and Computer Pools may offer some quieter moments). Since the Skyliner opened in 2019, Pop Century also became a top spot to rest your head at night since you can wake up in the morning, grab your Joffrey's, and hop in a gondola to get to Disney's Hollywood Studios and EPCOT — no buses needed.

If you want to stay in a particular decade area of the resort, you can try calling ahead of your visit or noting the request when you complete your online check-in. There's no guarantee that Cast Members can accommodate, but it's worth a shot. I especially like the '60s area. While it's by the largest (and thus loudest) pool, I'm usually awake before the pool opens and asleep long after it closes — and this area offers the shortest walk to the Skyliner, ideal for rope-dropping EPCOT.

LEFT: The Skyliner makes the trip easy — and fun — to get to EPCOT and Hollywood Studios. **PHOTO BY LAURIE SAPP** RIGHT: Find the Skyliner Station between Art of Animation and Pop Century. **PHOTO BY JUDD HELMS**

DISNEY'S ART OF ANIMATION RESORT
Best for Swimmers

Disney's Art of Animation is also conveniently located by the Skyliner (the *Finding Nemo* rooms give you the easiest access to the transportation system), but this resort is even more notable for its pools. In particular, AoA's feature pool — the Big Blue Pool — is the largest at Walt Disney World, holding 308,527 gallons. *Righteous!*

Another stand-out feature at Art of Animation: the themed rooms. You can get a *Little Mermaid* Standard Room (sleeps four adults), but larger families may want to spring for the *Finding Nemo*, *Cars*, or *Lion King* Family Suites. These themed rooms add extra magic to your stay, with colorful wall art, themed furniture, and creative details in the carpet, curtains, and bathrooms.

Regardless of where you stay — Pop Century or Art of Animation — you have easy access to its sister resort's cafeteria and pool bar. Cross Hourglass Lake to get to the other resort; you'll pass the Skyliner Station along the way.

ABOVE: Art of Animation has wonderful Family Suites. **PHOTO BY JUDD HELMS**

RIGHT: Nemo. That's a nice name. (And a big pool featuring the fish himself!) **PHOTO BY DANNY SHUSTER**

Yes, that's Sorcerer Mickey in the Fantasia pool, but fear not — Chernabog's nowhere to be found! **PHOTO BY DANNY SHUSTER**

DISNEY'S ALL-STAR MOVIES RESORT
Best for Classic Disney Movie Fans

Art of Animation isn't the only option for movie lovers, however, and AoA admittedly focuses on Disney Renaissance and Pixar films. Fans of classic Disney films may prefer a stay at Disney's All-Star Movies Resort. Here, you can explore some of your favorite Disney flicks through larger-than-life character statues, representing films such as *One Hundred and One Dalmatians*, *The Mighty Ducks*, *Toy Story*, *The Love Bug*, and *Fantasia*. The feature pool feels extra magical, as a Sorcerer Mickey statue looms above. (It's like you've stepped into Fantasmic!)

While All-Star Movies is less ideally situated than Art of Animation (AoA and Pop make it easy not only to get to Hollywood Studios and EPCOT but also to enjoy food and drinks at other Skyliner resorts), All-Star Movies *does* deliver the classic Disney character statues and signature theming at a lower price than AoA. You'll just have to bus everywhere if you don't have a car, even to nearby Animal Kingdom.

Perdita greets you at Disney's All-Star Movies Resort. **PHOTO BY JUDD HELMS**

Can't decide between Movies, Sports, and Music? Split the difference — Disney's All-Star Music Resort's between the other two, so you can resort hop with ease. **PHOTO BY JUDD HELMS**

DISNEY'S ALL-STAR MUSIC RESORT
Best for Big Families

All three All-Star Resorts feel similar — swap out some music notes for tennis rackets, and All-Star Music and Sports could be the same — but All-Star Music has one notable difference: Like Art of Animation, it offers Family Suites. This means bigger families on a budget should prioritize All-Star Music over Movies and Sports. Like at Art of Animation, the Family Suites at All-Star Music sleep six adults, but the All-Star versions are usually more affordable than the suites at AoA.

Another All-Stars plus: After a long day at the parks, the line for your resort bus might look long. If the nearby line for another All-Star Resort location is significantly shorter — and you don't mind some extra walking — switch lines. You'll likely get to the resort area faster, and you'll just need to follow the sidewalk north or south to your home resort for the night. All-Star Music is the ideal resort to stay for this strategy since it's in between Movies and Sports.

You might even say these Value Resorts rock... **PHOTO BY COURTNEY REYNOLDS**

DISNEY'S ALL-STAR SPORTS RESORT
Best for Visiting Sports Teams

Often the selection for visiting school sports teams due to its theming and proximity to the ESPN Wide World of Sports Complex, Disney's All-Star Sports is a great Value Resort option even if you don't have an athletic bone in your body. Though prices fluctuate, All-Stars Sports is typically the most affordable of the three All-Star Resorts, often making it the cheapest Value Resort at Walt Disney World. Plus, it's the only place on property where you can climb a staircase inside a cup of Coca-Cola.

During the busiest times of the day (park opening and closing), each All-Stars Resort typically runs its own buses. But at slower times, the resorts share buses — and All-Stars Sports has the upper hand here. By staying at All-Star Sports, you'll be the first group on the bus (and thus more likely to get a seat) and the first group off when you're heading back to your hotel.

LEFT: Disney's All-Stars Sports Resort has the least expensive hotel rooms on property, plus (RIGHT) you can climb to your room inside a giant cup of Coca-Cola! **PHOTOS BY JUDD HELMS**

BONUS: THE CAMPSITES AT DISNEY'S FORT WILDERNESS RESORT

The Cabins at Disney's Fort Wilderness Resort are technically a Moderate Resort and soon to get a DVC overhaul, but if you don't mind setting up a tent or hauling an RV (or having one delivered to your campsite!), you can stay at Fort Wilderness's campsites for a lot less.

Camping at Fort Wilderness has a lot of perks beyond the savings: Many campsite loops are pet-friendly, you can rent a golf cart to get around, and there's plenty to do — from archery and canoeing to horseback riding and swimming. Plus, you have access to great entertainment and dining, and a boat will take you straight to Magic Kingdom. 🐭

Feeling adventurous? Pitch your most magical tent and camp at Disney's Fort Wilderness Resort (they have RV spots, too, of course!). **PHOTO BY LAURIE SAPP**

Visit us online

Is planning part of the magic for you? Learn more about Value Resorts on our website!

Discovering New Magic

FAN-FAVORITE TRADITIONS AT WALT DISNEY WORLD

Walt Disney World is a place of tradition. For some of us, our first core memories are riding Dumbo, eating a Mickey bar, or seeing Cinderella Castle for the first time. Sharing those memories again and again with friends and family throughout our lives is part of the magic of this place we all call home.

We asked our fans what some of their favorite traditions are when they go to Walt Disney World. Here's what you had to say:

"We've never gone to Magic Kingdom without eating at Liberty Tree Tavern."

-Jessica L.

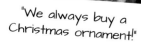

"Get a Mickey cookie when leaving Magic Kingdom. I love their cookies."

-Vicki L.

"We always buy a Christmas ornament!"

-Tyler F.

"We walk through the gate at Magic Kingdom and immediately head to Adventureland for a DOLE Whip."

-Frances M.

"Riding bikes through Fort Wilderness."

-Ken and Esther S.

PHOTOS BY WDW MAGAZINE PHOTOGRAPHY TEAM

"Meet at the statue. Ever since we were kids, we were told if we broke apart to go to different rides or if we got lost, to meet at the statue of Walt and Mickey. Now we're grown and have kids, and the rule still applies."

-Colt E.

"Photo of the welcome signs whenever we drive under them."

-Penny N.

"Always ride Dumbo in memory of riding it as a toddler with my Grammie (I'm over 50 now)."

-Gretchen H.

"Start each EPCOT day with a mimosa and chocolate croissant in France!"

-Jennifer R.

"Pictures with Mickey and Minnie."

-Annemarie W.

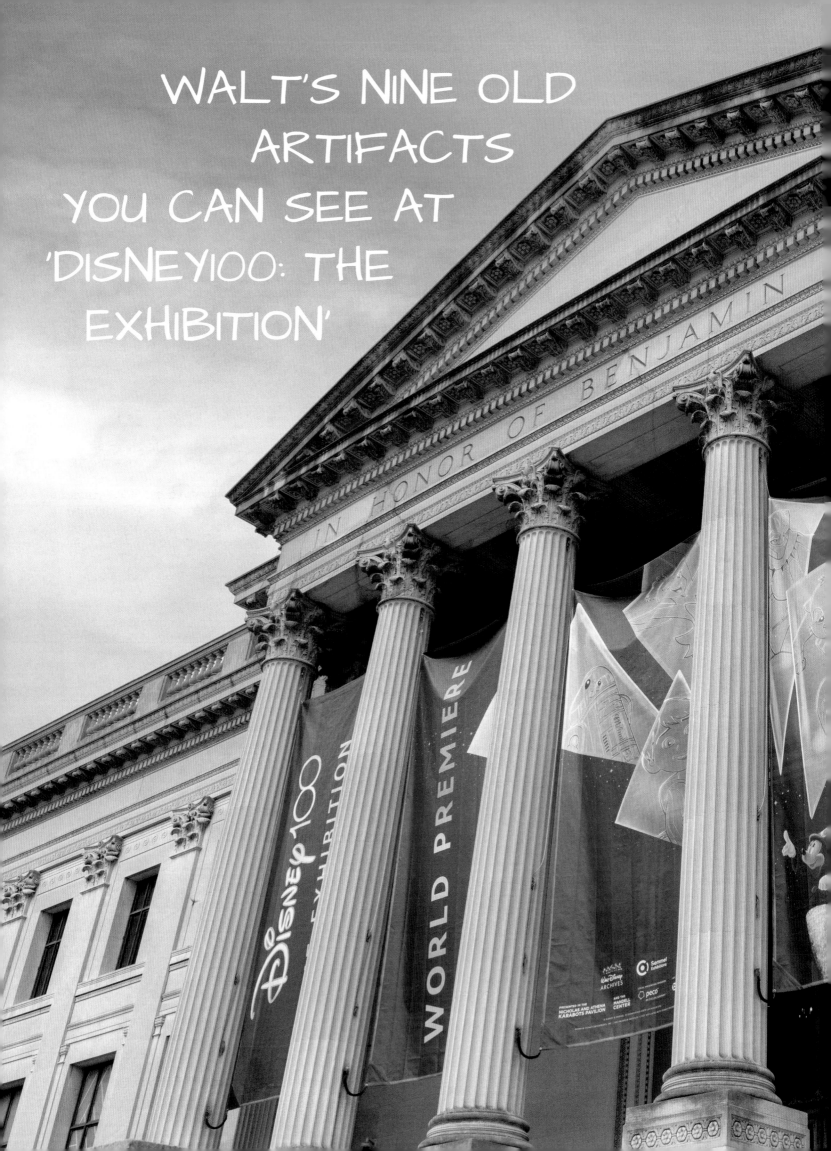

WALT'S NINE OLD ARTIFACTS YOU CAN SEE AT 'DISNEY100: THE EXHIBITION'

> "This incredible exhibit will take guests on a remarkable journey from those earliest days into Disney's dazzling future using seamless technology, a rich musical score, and - of course - treasures from the Walt Disney Archives collection."
>
> Becky Cline,
> *Director of the Walt Disney Archives*

Planning to visit the exhibit?
Find all the details on the blog

**TEXT AND PHOTOS
BY STEPHANIE SHUSTER**

Disney100: The Exhibition is a must-do for Disney megafans. As it travels to a roster of cities in the U.S. (we visited The Franklin Institute in Philadelphia) and Europe (the first stop is Olympiapark Munich in Germany) over the next five years, you'll be able to see hundreds of artifacts that hit a nostalgic note as only Disney can. Even the most serious fans will learn something new, whether it's about Walt's career before launching his own company, that *Lady and the Tramp* was based on a 1945 story in *Cosmopolitan* magazine, or that in the 1970s, a marketing campaign promoted Pooh for President.

DISNEY100: THE EXHIBITION INCLUDES 10 MULTIMEDIA GALLERIES TO EXPLORE:

- Where It All Began
- Where Do the Stories Come From?
- The Illusion of Life
- The Spirit of Adventure and Discovery
- The Magic of Sound and Music
- The World Around Us
- Innoventions
- Your Disney World
- The Wonder of Disney
- We Are Just Getting Started

You can explore countless items, from Captain Jack Sparrow's compass to Jimmie Dodd's Mousegetar to an automation bird in a cage from Walt's office, but here are a handful I was surprised (and delighted!) to see on show.

Coming soon to a city by you: Disney100: The Exhibition. **PHOTO BY DANNY SHUSTER**

THE LAUGH-O-GRAM MEGAPHONE

This megaphone was so much smaller than I imagined. Walt Disney used it when directing for Laugh-O-gram Films, Inc. (he animated for them, too!). Walt Disney Studios has redone many of the seven fairy tales in the Laugh-O-gram series in one fashion or another, but I still hold out hope Disney will remake *The Four Musicians of Bremen*, a childhood fave. During his time at the studio, Walt met Ub Iwerks and learned to flex his comedic muscles in directing an additional eight funny shorts that were a hybrid of animation and stop-motion cinematic styles.

THE ALICE COMEDIES

Building on what he learned at Laugh-O-gram, Walt ventured out to create his own series of silent shorts, marking the founding of The Walt Disney Company on Oct. 16, 1923 (hence the number in D23 Fan Club's name). Disney made 56 *Alice Comedies* between 1924 and 1927, again combining animation and live-action techniques (a technique still employed by Disney filmmakers today, although much more advanced). In the *Alice Comedies*, the entire world is a cartoon, with a live-action Alice. These films predate Mickey Mouse *and* Oswald the Lucky Rabbit. You can view clips under a mock marquee in the first gallery of the exhibition.

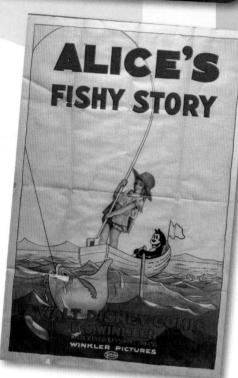

BEJEWELED BOOKS

More than 30 Disney films and shorts use the "storybook opening" trope to bring viewers into the action, and it all started with the prop storybook from *Snow White and the Seven Dwarfs*. It's on display at the exhibit, near artwork demonstrating the animation development with everything from charcoal sketches to watercolor backgrounds. One of the most show-stopping interactive displays is in the same gallery: a prop storybook from *Sleeping Beauty*, which guests can flip through to see projections of each scene on the wall.

A HAPPY SNOWMAN

As a huge theater nerd, I was delighted to see props and costume pieces from Disney's Broadway musicals. By far, the *coolest* was the Olaf toy puppet from *Frozen: The Musical*. Designed by Michael Curry (who also led production design on Rivers of Light in Disney's Animal Kingdom and co-designed the puppets for *The Lion King* on Broadway), this puppet was super-adorable to see up close, where we could appreciate all the handcrafted details, such as the button eyes and the wooden block legs.

THE NAUTILUS

Disney World fans share a nostalgia for Magic Kingdom's submarine attraction that closed in the 1990s. Disneyland still offers this fan-favorite ride, once based on Jules Verne's iconic tale, *20,000 Leagues Under the Sea*, but now themed after *Finding Nemo*. I'm not sure how many fans of the Magic Kingdom (and OG Disneyland) version are as passionate about the film as they are the attraction, but if you've never seen it (you should; it won Academy Awards for Best Special Effects and Best Art Direction/Set Decoration), you'll appreciate the ornate and rather large special-effects filming model at the exhibition.

ANCIENT JEDI TEXTS

I was expecting to see some droids, lightsabers, and costume pieces from *Star Wars* at *Disney100: The Exhibition*, but this was a movie prop I didn't see coming. the Ancient Jedi Texts is a huge, bound book used by Daisy Ridley (Rey) and Mark Hamill (Luke) in *The Last Jedi* and *The Rise of Skywalker*, and it sent shivers down my spine to see it in person. It was paired with a description of the painstaking process to create such a realistic artifact.

HERO HEAD COUNT

In addition to a full Black Panther suit, you can examine a collection of helmets used in the Marvel Cinematic Universe. It reminded me of seeing crowns and tiaras lined up in museums around Europe. In Philadelphia, we saw the metal mask Tony Stark first donned in a cave in *Iron Man*, Hope van Dyne's Wasp helmet from *Ant-Man and the Wasp*, Loki's iconic horned crown from *Thor: Ragnarok*, Ajak's helmet from *The Eternals*, and Star-Lord's face mask from the original *Guardians of the Galaxy*.

WALT'S PANTS

There were plenty of celebrity-worn costumes to see at the exhibition, but none were more interesting to me than the inclusion of a pair of gaucho pants given to Walt in Argentina in 1941. During this time in history, Walt and a handful of his artists traveled on a goodwill tour of South America to do research for future films like *Saludos Amigos* and to create a good neighborly relationship between North and South America.

FOLEY ART

In the music-themed gallery, we encountered a room tucked away showcasing sound effects and foley art, where I could have spent all day. The main feature was a series of stations where you could pick up an audio receiver and listen to the sound effects being made to correspond with animation on screen. A few recognizable pieces were a whistle used in *Steamboat Willie*, a glass bottle that stood in for the sound of pickaxes in the diamond mine in *Snow White*, and chimes to communicate Tinker Bell's movements. But far more intriguing were the unnamed, homemade contraptions created by Disney Legend and sound effects artist Jimmy Macdonald. He made hundreds of Rube Goldberg-like devices from everyday objects such as sticks and rubber tubing, producing an impressive archive of sound effects for Disney's motion pictures. 🐭

This Is What Dreams Are Made Of: The Disney Dreamers Academy

By Alessandra Sferlazza

The March 26, 2023 Disney Dreamers Academy commencement ceremony. **PHOTO BY CHARLENE MORRISON**

The Disney Dreamers Academy kick-off parade.

PHOTO BY CHARLENE MORRISON

One hundred high schoolers march behind drumline Mickey into a convention room at Disney's Coronado Springs as the audience cheers. Among them are students who dedicate their free time planting trees, aspiring engineers and artists, and teenage business owners who donate some of their profits to charity. These carefully selected students are about to embark on a long weekend of learning, bonding, and fun at the Walt Disney World Resort.

Welcome to the Disney Dreamers Academy.

The purpose of this program, first held in 2008, is to foster and inspire the dreams of students from underrepresented communities. Each Disney Dreamer (and their chaperone) spends a long weekend at Walt Disney World Resort, participating in workshops, sessions, and deep dives to help set them up for success. For many, this marks their first visit to Walt Disney World.

The Walt Disney Company invited *WDW Magazine* to shadow the 2023 Disney Dreamers Academy (DDA). After the four-day event, during which we witnessed the energy and passion of these students, we feel confident their dreams can fuel a brighter tomorrow.

DISNEY DREAMERS ACADEMY PARADE

On the first day of the Disney Dreamers Academy, the students met their celebrity ambassador, Halle Bailey. Bailey participated in the weekend's activities, starting with the Disney Dreamers Academy Parade.

In this parade, the Disney Dreamers marched down Main Street, U.S.A. while guests and chaperones cheered. After the parade, the students explored Magic Kingdom with their new friends and got a special preview of TRON: Lightcycle / Run, which had not yet opened to most guests.

Know someone who could benefit from the program? Disney's currently looking for its Class of 2024. Encourage your future Dreamer to apply by Oct. 31, 2023.

Pluto and the Dreamers march down Main Street, U.S.A.

PHOTO BY ALESSANDRA SFERLAZZA

CAREER DEEP DIVES

During the long weekend, students worked with professionals in their desired fields, giving them hands-on experience during the learning process. For instance, students who hope to become Imagineers participated in a career deep dive led by current Imagineers, including an Imagineer who worked on the "show element" of *Guardians of the Galaxy*: Cosmic Rewind. This specific session walked Disney Dreamers through the process of creating a new attraction or land at the parks from concept to completion. In groups, the students then built attraction models using arts and crafts materials, including pipe cleaners, masking tape, card stock, and marbles.

Although Disney runs this program, the company opens it to more than aspiring Imagineers. During another career deep dive focused on creating and composing music, Grammy Award-winning musician H.E.R. joined the Disney Dreamers to offer advice about the music industry. She also surprised the students with autographed guitars. Other deep dives allowed the Dreamers to work alongside industry leaders in their desired career fields, including law, STEM, film and television, writing, and fashion.

Items from the DDA Imagineering deep dive, which helped Dreamers understand how much detail goes into creating everything at Walt Disney World. **PHOTOS BY ALESSANDRA SFERLAZZA**

WHERE ARE THEY NOW? ALUMNI STORIES

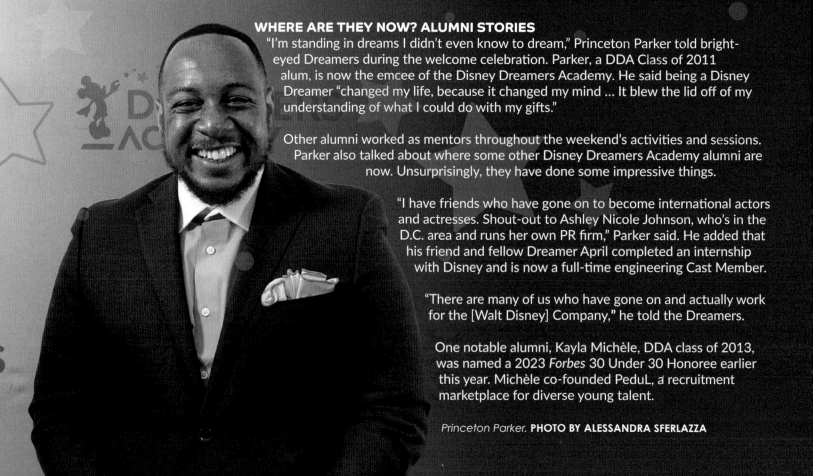

"I'm standing in dreams I didn't even know to dream," Princeton Parker told bright-eyed Dreamers during the welcome celebration. Parker, a DDA Class of 2011 alum, is now the emcee of the Disney Dreamers Academy. He said being a Disney Dreamer "changed my life, because it changed my mind ... It blew the lid off of my understanding of what I could do with my gifts."

Other alumni worked as mentors throughout the weekend's activities and sessions. Parker also talked about where some other Disney Dreamers Academy alumni are now. Unsurprisingly, they have done some impressive things.

"I have friends who have gone on to become international actors and actresses. Shout-out to Ashley Nicole Johnson, who's in the D.C. area and runs her own PR firm," Parker said. He added that his friend and fellow Dreamer April completed an internship with Disney and is now a full-time engineering Cast Member.

"There are many of us who have gone on and actually work for the [Walt Disney] Company," he told the Dreamers.

One notable alumni, Kayla Michèle, DDA class of 2013, was named a 2023 *Forbes* 30 Under 30 Honoree earlier this year. Michèle co-founded PeduL, a recruitment marketplace for diverse young talent.

Princeton Parker. **PHOTO BY ALESSANDRA SFERLAZZA**

SPEAKER SESSIONS

Industry leaders and celebrity mentors are a huge component of the Disney Dreamers Academy. Throughout the weekend, these guests addressed the Dreamers during speaker sessions, sharing their stories and offering advice on following dreams, making a path for themselves, and finding the courage to believe in their aspirations.

Some of the industry leaders included Essence CEO Caroline Wanga; Essence Vice President of Sales Alicia Richarsdon; Dr. Terrence Ferguson and Dr. Vernard Hodges of National Geographic's *Critter Fixers: Country Vets*; ABC's Mike Muse; and stylists Jerome LaMaar and Misa Hylton. LaMaar and Hylton hosted the

During the "Put You On" Image Makeover Session, professional stylists worked with eight dreamers, who later showed off their new look on the runway. **PHOTO BY ALESSANDRA SFERLAZZA**

"Put You On" Image Makeover Session, during which eight students received a style makeover, then showed off their new looks on the runway.

LaMaar and Hylton spoke about the importance of creating a personal brand and image for yourself through fashion. They also discussed how personal style and branding aren't communicated through clothing alone, but through integrity and a person's values.

Among the celebrity mentors were Marsai Martin of ABC's *Black-ish*, Marvel's Dominique Thorne, H.E.R., Jalyn Emil Hall, Amir and Amari O'Neil, Questlove, and Halle Bailey. These celebrities shared advice and encouraging words about staying strong and believing in yourself while chasing your dreams in music, film, and television.

AN INSPIRING "SEE YOU LATER"

On the last day of the academy, Disney held a commencement ceremony celebrating the Dreamers. The emotional send-off featured many speakers from the weekend, who all reaffirmed the values and lessons of the sessions, activities, and events.

Halle Bailey spoke to the Dreamers last and reinforced that "this is a momentous occasion" for the Disney Dreamers — but also only the beginning for them, too. She closed with encouraging words: "It is time to make those dreams a reality."

Halle Bailey spoke to the Dreamers, offering final notes of inspiration. **PHOTO BY CHARLENE MORRISON**

Mickey Mouse joined the DDA's Chief Executive Champion, Tracey Powell, on stage for one last "see you later," and distributed class rings to the students. Each chaperone placed the ring on their Dreamer's finger as a way to honor their love, support, and encouragement — and their commitment to the Dreamer's future.

And what a bright future it will be. ✦

A DREAM IS A WISH YOUR HEART MAKES... MEET THESE DREAMERS WHO DID JUST THAT!

It's not goodbye, it's "see you real soon!" **PHOTO BY CHARLENE MORRISON**

PARK PRO TURNED PARENT: ADVICE FOR FIRST-TIMERS *WITH KIDS!*

TEXT BY JENNIFER DRAHER
PHOTOS BY CLIFF WANG

Even if you're a seasoned Annual Passholder, visiting the parks for the first time as a new parent will feel like a whole new world. Here are a few tips to keep in mind for your first Disney outing as a family.

FIND THE BABY CARE CENTERS

Familiarize yourself with the Baby Care Center in each park. They offer private nursing rooms with rocking chairs, high chairs, changing stations, and kitchen space to wash bottles or heat baby food. While most restrooms throughout the resort have changing tables (bring a travel pack of bleach wipes), none compare to the clean, welcoming, and fully staffed Baby Care Centers.

You can also purchase formula, diapers, sunscreen, and other essentials. If you bring more than one child, you'll love the family restrooms and the fact that there's always a movie playing in the waiting area.

PRO TIP: Incorporate napping and changing into rider switches when possible. Instead of waiting 45 minutes or more in a long line with your mini-Mouseketeer, head to the Baby Care Center to recharge.

STROLLERS

Don't skimp on the stroller! Yes, this is an extra cost, but it's more than a magic (carpet) ride for the kids — it doubles as a recliner where they can nap. That is, if you pick the right one.

I've always preferred the third-party stroller rental companies that deliver strollers to the resorts because they have more options with padded seats and snack or souvenir storage bins underneath. Plus, when you're exhausted at the end of the day, the stroller carries your sleeping toddler back to your room. You'll have to fold down strollers for most transportation, but no need to on the Skyliner — it fits right inside!

Taking a toddler to Walt Disney World? Heed these tips from a seasoned pro!

Don't sleep on third-party strollers, which can offer more features for kiddos — and you (think extra places to stash souvenirs)!

PRO TIP: Worried about getting lost in a sea of strollers, especially in Fantasyland? Personalize yours with a sign or decoration so it's easy to spot. Just skip the balloons, at least at Animal Kingdom. Balloons aren't permitted there because of conservation efforts.

COMFY CLOTHES AND PRIORITY PHOTOS

It's so tempting to buy the fancy dresses for your little princess. Though they make for a magical photo op, the hand wash-only, heavy nylon — with glitter that sheds like pixie dust — also gets itchy and hot. These outfits aren't always practical in the parks, so save them for Halloween and avoid an epic meltdown. Turn to Jane, Etsy, or Amazon for more breathable princess-inspired dresses your kids will love.

It's OK to ask a Cast Member to take a family photo with your phone — they're happy to do it!

Plan to get the priority photo moments out of the way when you first arrive at the parks, while everyone still looks their best. If there are characters your kids want to meet, earlier in the day is the way to go — lines swell after lunch. That frees you up to sneak out for an afternoon nap, too.

PRO TIP: Ask Cast Members to take pictures so the entire family gets in the shot. These memories will last a lifetime, so don't cut yourself out of them just because you're used to standing behind the lens. You can also ask them to take photos with your phone.

HYDRATE

Spending all day in the sun — and taking literally thousands of steps — can make anyone cranky, but especially little ones. Make sure you all stay hydrated (and coated in sunscreen) throughout the day. Water is obviously the top choice, but popsicles and DOLE Whips will do the trick, too.

If you want a meltdown-free nighttime spectacular, don't forget to schedule a nap.

LET THE KIDS LEAD

It's always smart to curate your park days to get the most out of them. That said, pick your battles with the kids. If they don't do well waiting for character greetings at the park, look for dining reservations where you can eat while meeting your faves. Just know going in that you may have to abandon your plans and take cues from the kids.

However the day takes shape, make the best of your new family's time together in the Most Magical Place on Earth. 🐭

CHARACTER MAGIC: Moana

BY TRISHA DAAB

KNOW THE WAY... to meet Moana at Disney's Animal Kingdom. Find her at Character Landing in Discovery Island, right outside the entrance to DinoLand U.S.A.

Hei Hei and Pua aren't with Moana, but you'll find beautiful banners around the meet-and-greet area featuring different characters and symbols from the film.

YOU'RE WELCOME to see Moana during the daytime. Check the My Disney Experience app; she often sets sail before 5 p.m.

KNOW WHO YOU ARE: Introduce yourself to Moana, and then ask what her favorite boat snacks are or the best way to have a coconut.

SHINY things may be Tamatoa's preference, but Moana loves the water. Ask her to autograph a beach-themed snow globe or giant seashell. Or show her you know the way and ask her to sign a map of Animal Kingdom.

SHOW HOW FAR YOU'LL GO: Head to Magic Kingdom to see the Moana moments in the nighttime show Happily Ever After. Sing along to the inspirational sequence featuring the song "How Far I'll Go" during the *Moana* projections on the castle and down Main Street, U.S.A.

PHOTO ©DISNEY

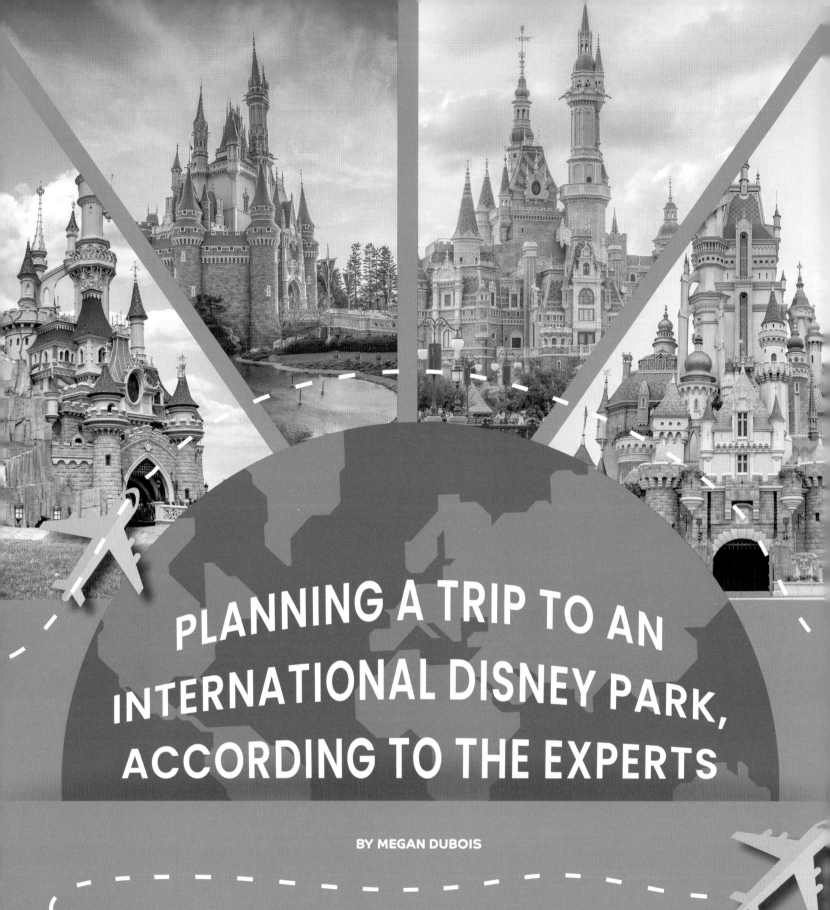

PLANNING A TRIP TO AN INTERNATIONAL DISNEY PARK, ACCORDING TO THE EXPERTS

BY MEGAN DUBOIS

Walking through the turnstiles at all the Disney Parks around the world: It's the ultimate bucket-list achievement — yet often a logistical challenge — for mega Disney fans. Planning a trip to a domestic Disney Resort like Walt Disney World or Disneyland may come as second nature for avid Disney guests, but the international parks have their own quirks that make planning a trip more difficult.

Up for the challenge? *WDW Magazine* spoke with travel experts — including Disney Travel Agents from Destinations To Travel *and* Asia parks authority, Chris Nilghe — to get their top tips for planning a trip to Disneyland Paris Resort, Tokyo Disney Resort, Shanghai Disney Resort, and Hong Kong Disneyland Resort.

WHAT YOU SHOULD DO FIRST IF YOU WANT TO VISIT AN INTERNATIONAL PARK

"Of course, contact your travel agent," says Katie Prevot, a travel agent with Destinations To Travel.

You'll also want to ensure your passport is up to date and not set to expire anytime soon. According to the U.S. State Department, some countries require that passports be valid at least *six months* beyond your travel dates. Downloading Duolingo or Babbel and brushing up on a new language doesn't hurt, either.

Unlike the American Disney Parks, the international resorts all have different booking windows and packages. Which of the four resorts you want to visit will impact how far in advance you should start planning your trip and booking elements such as park tickets, hotel rooms, and dining reservations.

PLANING FOR DISNEYLAND PARIS RESORT

Disneyland Paris is often considered Disney's most beautiful park, with its charming Main Street, U.S.A. and pastel-pink castle. The resort always looks stunning in photos, but having an Instagram-worthy trip at Disneyland Paris requires some planning.

The weather in France can be finicky, with overcast skies in the fall and winter, and rain in spring and summer. Accept the reality of weather now: It's unlikely you'll have multiple days in a row of perfect weather at Disneyland Paris. If you're looking for the most ideal weather for those perfect park pics, Katie says to go between November and April. You'll avoid the summer crowds — *and* the summer heat.

"Make sure to check the country's local holidays, as well," she says. Such holidays, like Bastille Day on July 14, can impact crowd levels at the parks as well as ease of transportation to and from the parks.

You can book packages for Disneyland Paris almost a full year in advance, with a deposit due at the time of booking. The final payment is due about two weeks prior to your arrival date. If you don't want to deal with figuring out meals abroad, Disneyland Paris offers packages with dining options, though character dining is an upgrade.

Prepare for some culture shocks when you arrive in Paris. Customer service in Europe, for instance, can be more direct.

"Customer service is very objective [and] task oriented," says Angie Baycura, a travel planner with Destinations To Travel. Angie also says that while most Cast Members speak English, it's wise to learn a few basic phrases in French to get a conversation going.

As for can't-miss experiences at Disneyland Paris? Both Katie and Angie agree that Crush's Coaster is the one attraction not to skip. And don't forget to journey under the castle to discover the dragon lurking in the mist.

Sleeping Beauty Castle at Disneyland Paris… plus the dragon who lies beneath. **PHOTOS BY NICK BARESE**

PLANNING FOR TOKYO DISNEY RESORT

The best time to visit Tokyo Disney Resort depends on your own preferences, according to Chris Nilghe, owner of TDR Explorer and author behind the *TDR Explorer Guide to Tokyo Disney Resort*. According to Chris, March and April have the best weather, but can be busy because that's also peak cherry blossom season. If you want low crowds and great weather, mid-May through June is nice. October through November brings Halloween and Christmas into the parks, but it's also typhoon season, which can throw a huge wrench in travel plans.

Preparing for travel requirements to an Asian country and actually booking the tickets may seem daunting, but Chris says it's pretty straightforward.

"If you hold a U.S. or Canadian passport, you're given a 90-day visitor visa on arrival into Japan, so there's nothing for you to do ahead of time in that case," Chris tells *WDW Magazine*.

"As for booking Tokyo Disney Resort," he adds, "hotels are three months out and park tickets are two months. There's not a lot to pre-book when it comes to Tokyo Disney Resort."

Unlike at the American and European Disney Parks, guests shouldn't assume that Japanese Cast Members speak English.

"You will encounter those who speak English, but more often than not, people won't, or [they'll] know only a little," he says. "Knowing a few pleasantries goes a long way, too — people do appreciate it."

Once you're on the ground in Tokyo, you'll notice some cultural differences right away. But maybe the biggest you'll spot while actually inside the parks is that people sit down for parades, especially when up close.

"For Tokyo Disneyland and Tokyo DisneySea, there are sitting areas that have some of the best seats in the house," Chris says. "Even during the show, you can still sit. This makes it easier for everyone to see the show who is further back and has to stand."

There's *a lot* to do across the two parks at Tokyo Disney Resort. For guests who can't see it all, Chris recomments prioritizing Journey to the Center of the Earth at Tokyo DisneySea and Enchanted Tales of Beauty and the Beast at Tokyo Disneyland.

Cinderella Castle at Tokyo Disneyland is a clone of the one at Walt Disney World — with the classic paint colors. **PHOTO BY HIROKI HASEGAWA**

ABOVE: Mysterious Island at Tokyo Disney Resort's DisneySea lets you explore the world of Captain Nemo. BOTTOM LEFT: Journey to the Center of the Earth is a Tokyo DisneySea must. **PHOTOS BY ALEXANDER SEMENCIC** | *BOTTOM RIGHT: Enchanted Tales of Beauty and the Beast at Tokyo Disneyland is another don't-miss experience.* **PHOTO BY TDR EXPLORER**

The Enchanted Storybook Castle awaits you at Shanghai Disney Resort. **PHOTO BY HIROKI HASEGAWA**

ABOVE: The recently renovated Castle of Magical Dreams at Hong Kong Disneyland. **PHOTO BY TRACY AU** *BELOW: Hong Kong Disneyland's Mystic Manor offers an eerie take on Haunted Mansion.* **PHOTO BY BRIAN SHIH**

PLANNING FOR SHANGHAI DISNEY RESORT

Shanghai Disney Resort is the newest international Disney Park and offers a wide range of rides and activities. As with the other Disney Parks, guests should keep in mind major national holidays, like Chinese New Year (late January or early February) and National Day (Oct. 1), when planning a trip to Shanghai Disney Resort. Crowds can grow during these times.

You can purchase one- or two-day tickets for Shanghai Disneyland. For single-day tickets, you can also add on a selection of Disney Premier Access sets, which act like pre-paid Lightning Lane options.

Previous to TRON Lightcycle / Run's opening at Magic Kingdom at Walt Disney World, the ride was a must-do at Shanghai Disneyland. If you've experienced TRON in Florida and are pressed for time, our travel experts recommend prioritizing Pirates of the Caribbean: Battle for the Sunken Treasure, which is a high-tech version of the classic ride.

PLANNING FOR HONG KONG DISNEYLAND RESORT

Although it's Disney's smallest park, Hong Kong Disneyland is well worth the visit. Plan your trip around the weather, major holidays, and when kids are out of school in Asia. The best time to visit for mild temperatures and low crowds is April and May since there aren't any holiday activities at the park and kids are still in school.

Getting to the resort is easy. You can take the Mass Transit Railway (MTR), but the hotels are a short (and affordable) taxi ride from the airport. Transportation isn't the only easy thing about Hong Kong: English-speaking guests may be surprised to find that Cast Members commonly speak English, and many shows and attractions offer dialogue in English as well.

You can buy one- or two-day tickets for the park online. Don't let the size of the park fool you: If this is your one-and-only Hong Kong Disneyland trip, get the two-day ticket. Highlights at the park include Mystic Manor (an eerie take on Haunted Mansion), the Iron Man Experience, and the Hong Kong Disneyland Railroad. Next month, World of Frozen opens at the park — and it's sure to be a top reason to visit in 2024. 🖤

BE A GLOBAL ARMCHAIR TRAVELER WITH US ON YOUTUBE.

ENTER
THE GRID

PHOTO BY CLIFF WANG

HUNDRED-ACRE FEAST

BY BROOKE MCDONALD

f you find yourself in Magic Kingdom with a rumbly in your tumbly and a hankering for hugs, it's time for an "expotition," as Winnie the Pooh would say, to one of Walt Disney World's oldest and most beloved restaurants. Situated off Main Street, U.S.A., The Crystal Palace is home to a fan-favorite buffet, hosted by the Hundred-Acre Wood gang.

A MAGIC KINGDOM STAPLE

Crystal Palace opened with Magic Kingdom on Oct. 1, 1971, offering what my 1986 Magic Kingdom Guide Book described as "buffeteria-style service" of "breakfast, luncheon, dinner, exotic salads," and "100% Colombian Coffee."

It wasn't until 1996 that Disney introduced character and buffet dining, along with a revised name: "The Crystal Palace: A Buffet with Character." While the menu and entertainment evolved, the restaurant looks much the same today as it did on opening day.

Inspired by Victorian greenhouses of the late 1800s, the restaurant gets its name from the original "Crystal Palace," an iron-and-glass structure in London by botanist and greenhouse builder Joseph Paxton. The original housed The Great Exhibition of 1851 and inspired numerous future structures, also dubbed "crystal palaces."

"The design of The Crystal Palace marked the latest incarnation of a unique Victorian glass conservatory style, which includes Kew Gardens in England and the Conservatory of Flowers at Golden Gate Park in San Francisco," says a Walt Disney Imagineering spokesperson. "Unlike its predecessors, this conservatory houses more dining tables than exotic plant species, offering one of the most elegant dining experiences at Magic Kingdom."

The building design also softens the visual transition from Main Street into Adventureland.

"The restaurant uses carefully curated turn-of-the-century aesthetics blended with lush tropical foliage to serve as the gateway to inspired visions of Adventureland architecture nearest the hub," the WDI spokesperson says.

Inside, guests are greeted by a centerpiece display of tropical foliage, florals, and character topiaries beneath a "homemade" misspelled banner: "Welcome to Our Friendship Day Celebrashun!"

By day, natural light pours in through the foyer's glass-domed ceiling and colorful stained-glass windows throughout the restaurant. The dining room is lined with Victorian arches and adorned with hanging plants and decorative lights.

By day, light spills into the restaurant through the glass-domed ceiling.
PHOTO BY ABBY RICHARDSON

The flowers peeking out from the exotic plants seem to add a bright cast to Eeyore's ennui. **PHOTO BY ABBY RICHARDSON**

You'll get a commemorative card to remember the "celebrashun" (and don't worry, Crystal Palace does better with the food than Pooh does with the spelling!). **PHOTO BY ABBY RICHARDSON**

WHEN TO GO

The restaurant serves a buffet-style breakfast, lunch, and dinner, with service running continuously from open to close — though reservations (highly recommended) will be specifically for breakfast, lunch, or dinner.

Food offerings at lunch and dinner are about the same, as is the price — $59 per adult, plus tax and gratuity; $38 per child (age 3-9). Breakfast is less expensive — $45 per adult; $29 per child (3-9). You'll see the same characters all day, so visiting at breakfast is a great way to save.

To stretch our meal spend further, we book the last breakfast reservation of the day (10:45 a.m.), and make it a brunch that fills us up until dinner. An added bonus, at 11 a.m., Cast Members close half of the breakfast buffet and replace it with lunch foods, so from 11 to 11:30 a.m., you can enjoy dishes from both meals. An alternate timing tip: Book the first breakfast reservation of the morning, typically an hour before park opening. You'll get a head start on your day and a chance to grab photos in a quiet park.

ON THE MENU

The fare is "traditional American," but there are some unique dishes you won't find elsewhere at Walt Disney World.

"We serve classic breakfast dishes that appeal to guests of all ages, such as Churro Mickey Waffles, Chocolate Chip Pound Cake French Toast, and Cheesy Potato Casserole," says Magic Kingdom Park's Culinary Director James O'Donnell.

We'd come here just for Churro Mickey Waffles — a plussed version of the Disney breakfast classic only served here.

More standard offerings include Traditional Roast Beef Hash, Biscuits and Sausage Gravy, bacon, scrambled eggs, and pancakes. You'll also find continental staples like croissants, pastries, fresh fruit, oatmeal, yogurt, granola, and smoked salmon with capers.

Another unique favorite is the Puffy French Toast. Served at the Pooh's Corner Children's Buffet, a shorter-height lineup of kid-friendly dishes such as pancakes and plain Mickey-shaped Waffles, these fluffy, fried fritters are coated in cinnamon and sugar and taste delicious on their own or dunked in maple syrup.

Other can't-miss sweet treats include the Blackberry-Streusel Coffee Cake and the Signature Breakfast Lasagna.

ABOVE: Book a 10:45 reservation and from 11-11:30 a.m., you can eat breakfast and lunch. **PHOTO BY ABBY RICHARDSON** | *BELOW: Mickey-shaped waffles, but make it churro.* **PHOTO BY BROOKE MCDONALD**

If savory is more your style, there are egg-based frittatas and a plant-based Keralan Tofu Curry that wowed the meat-eaters at our table. Guests with food allergies and other dietary restrictions can talk to the chef for recommendations and modifications.

Some dishes are so popular they're staples for all three meals.

"Our Shrimp Creole and Smoked Cheddar Grits are served all day long and are guest favorites," O'Donnell says.

When it's time for lunch and dinner, Cast Members replace the chilled breakfast spread with colorful salad ingredients, artisanal meats and cheeses, fresh rolls, and Peel 'n Eat Shrimp. Main courses include something for everyone — including Country Fried Chicken with Black Pepper Gravy and Honey-Tabasco Sauce (a huge hit at our table), Oven-roasted Chicken, Italian Sausage, Seared Mahi Mahi, and Spinach Ravioli. Vegetarians have plenty of options, but could make a meal out of sides like Cheesy Broccoli, Roasted Marble Potatoes, and Glazed Rainbow Carrots.

O'Donnell recommends the carving station: "We are proud of our spit-roasted Prime Rib cooked over an open fire and carved-to-order."

On the Kids' Buffet, less-adventurous eaters are set with favorites like Crispy Chicken Nuggets, Creamy Macaroni & Cheese, Miniature Beef Quesadillas, and Cheesy Pizza Bread.

And if anyone has managed to save room for dessert, taster-sized portions make it easier to sample a few treats like French Silk Cupcakes, Blueberry Domes, S'mores Tarts, and Butterscotch Pudding, all made fresh daily by the pastry team.

Juice, coffee, tea, milk, and soft drinks are included, but grown-ups in the mood for an adult beverage can order beer, wine, and specialty cocktails for an additional charge.

HIP, HIP, POOH-RAY!
The food is great, but hugs and high fives from Winnie the Pooh and his pals are the bigger draw. During your meal, you'll

ABOVE: Tigger's always happy to see everyone, no matter what time of day! BELOW: So are all the characters — so it doesn't matter which meal you choose, you'll get to meet them all! **PHOTOS BY ABBY RICHARDSON**

typically meet Pooh, Piglet, Tigger, and Eeyore, who will each visit your table.

There are no Disney PhotoPass photographers available, but a character attendant can snap a photo with your phone. Characters will sign autographs, and you'll also get a pre-printed souvenir autograph card.

Characters rotate in order, and if you miss one, you have to wait for them to make a full round of the tables and return. Prioritize waiting at your table for characters and work your buffet trips around them. Ask your server if you're not sure when to go.

Stamp Your Culinary Passport at These Bountiful Buffets

Buffets help unadventurous eaters challenge their palates with a little taste of everything. Our fans may have voted for Crystal Palace as their favorite buffet, but these other buffets, which serve authentic cuisine from far-flung destinations along with a heaping helping of theming and entertainment, should also be on your list.

Crystal Palace softens the transition from Main Street, U.S.A. to Adventureland. **PHOTO BY ABBY RICHARDSON**

Boma — Flavors of Africa

It's a bit off the beaten path, but this top-rated buffet at Disney's Animal Kingdom Lodge is worth the trek. With flavors from more than 50 different African countries, alongside familiar favorites like Mickey-shaped (and Simba-shaped!) Waffles for breakfast and Macaroni & Cheese for dinner, Boma serves a winning balance of familiar and exotic options. Oenophiles, don't miss the South Africa-heavy wine list; sugar fiends, don't miss the Zebra Domes for dessert (trust me).

Biergarten

It's always Oktoberfest at this lively indoor restaurant in EPCOT's Germany Pavilion. Dine in perpetual twilight at communal tables in a charming German village square as you enjoy traditional German fare. Hoist a stein of classic German beer, and sing (and dance!) along with the traditional Bavarian polka band.

Tusker House Restaurant

More African-inspired flavors are on the menu at this beloved character dining destination in the Africa area of Disney's Animal Kingdom. Donald, Daisy, Mickey, and Goofy host this lively meal in their safari gear, celebrating their latest far-flung adventures.

Speaking of servers, Crystal Palace has some of the longest-tenured Cast Members you'll encounter at Disney World, so show them some love, too.

"There are many talented Cast Members at The Crystal Palace, many of whom were with us when The Crystal Palace: A Buffet with Character opened over 25 years ago!" says Crystal Palace Proprietor Dawn Gullia. ❤

Pin of the Month

NAME: Winnie the Pooh Balloons - Pooh
EDITION SIZE: Limited Edition 400
YEAR RELEASED: 2022
ORIGINAL RETAIL PRICE: $24.95

Not even a blustery day can keep Winnie the Pooh from peacefully floating on this fuschia sandblast balloon in the clouds. Released online right after Valentine's Day by Disney Studio Store Hollywood, this pin set contains eight Winnie the Pooh characters — Pooh, Tigger, Piglet, Eeyore, Rabbit, Kanga, Roo, and Owl — all with different color balloons.

These pin-on-pin designs set the clouds behind the characters and their balloons to create a floating effect with extra dimension. While Pooh is actually lying on top of his balloon, which seems in character for this silly old bear, six of the other characters in the set happily (or unhappily — *hi, Eeyore!*) hang from their strings while floating. Owl, of course, carries his string in his beak as he soars.

But why is Pooh clinging to a balloon in the first place? We can't be sure, but we suspect Pooh thought traveling by balloon was a great way to search tall honey trees for a sweet snack!

TOP 6

WDW MAGAZINE MEMES

We love our fan base on social media and always enjoy creating memes that resonate with fellow Walt Disney World fanatics. These are some of our most-liked and most-shared memes across our social channels.

JOIN US ON FACEBOOK FOR MORE GREAT MEMES.

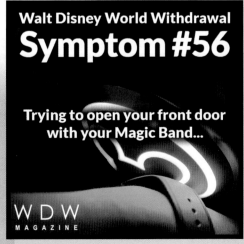

*Less popular — but ever-as-tasty —
snacks often get overlooked in favor
of DOLE Whips. We ask: Why not both?*
PHOTO BY BRETT SVENSON

Secret Snacking

The Disney Snacks Everyone Knows About —
and Lesser-Known Alternatives

By Josie Maida

From the Mickey's Premium Ice Cream Bar to Mickey Pretzels to Mickey-shaped Waffles, everyone seems to share the same Disney snack obsessions. Understandably so: These are delicious park staples. And picking between them is tough: Ahead of this issue, we asked fans to choose between a DOLE Whip and a Mickey's Premium Ice Cream Bar as their favorite Disney snack — and the vote resulted in a tie!

But Disney snacks go far beyond the tried-and-true eats. For every park-day favorite, there's a lesser-known snack that's sometimes even better. As a Disney foodie expert, let me take you through a whole new world of flavor awaiting you at Walt Disney World.

STUFFED PRETZELS

Mickey Pretzels and the less-ubiquitous Simba Pretzels (sometimes found at Disney's Animal Kingdom) are delicious and adorable. But unless these simple and classic treats are smothered in bright yellow cheese sauce or chocolatey dip, they can taste a little plain, especially in a place filled with decadent delights. If you're on the hunt for a richer pretzel experience, Disney has the dough to make it happen.

At The Lunching Pad in Magic Kingdom's Tomorrowland, you can find the Cream Cheese Warm Stuffed Pretzel, which has a sweet, thick cream cheese filling. Magic Kingdom also delivers a more savory experience with the Pepper Jack Pretzel at the Cheshire Cafe. This pretzel, baked with jalapeño bread, has a bit of a kick. Both stuffed pretzels cost $7.49, same as the classic character pretzels.

ABOVE: The Cream Cheese Warm Stuffed Pretzel flies under most people's radar. **PHOTO BY JUDD HELMS**

MICKEY MOUSE ICE CREAM

If you've been in a Disney Park for more than five minutes, you've likely seen a Mickey's Premium Ice Cream Bar: a wooden popsicle stick supporting a Mickey-shaped block of creamy vanilla ice cream enrobed in a chocolatey coating. And they're delicious. This simplistic treat truly deserves the fanfare it gets: The bars really are *that* good.

And in the great Disney snack debate, fans usually have strong feelings about this ice cream bar and its cousin, the Mickey's Premium Ice Cream Sandwich. That doesn't leave a whole lot of love for other incredible frozen treats found around the parks.

If you're looking for something new, and a bit more customizable, head over to the Plaza Ice Cream Parlor in Magic Kingdom for a Mickey Mouse cup or cone. Here, you can get a scoop or two of ice cream in any flavor you want, served in a cup or a cone — pretty standard for an ice cream shop, of course. But this is Disney, so the magic doesn't end there. The ice cream shop can add two small chocolate disks to the top scoop of your frozen confection to create a Mickey-shaped treat, similar to the popular packaged snacks, only *these* customized snacks might look cuter and taste more delicious.

ABOVE: A fan favorite, the Mini Mickey Sink Sundae tempts taste buds of ice cream fans. BELOW: At Plaza Ice Cream Parlor, you can "make it Mickey" with two yummy chocolate disks.

PHOTOS BY LAURIE SAPP

WAFFLE SANDWICHES

Mickey-shaped food is a staple of any Disney trip, especially when you start your day with a hearty helping of malted Mickey-shaped Waffles. Golden brown and fluffy, these breakfast delights appear on menus at Disney Parks around the globe in a full array of sizes. While these waffles will cure my morning cravings, they're not my favorite waffle at Walt Disney World.

So what is? Two words: Waffle. Sandwiches. These delicious treats (or *meals*, really) take Disney's fresh-cooked waffles to a whole new level. The smell of Sleepy Hollow alone will draw you in as you head toward Fantasyland.

While the Mickey-shaped waffle is more crisp on the outside, Sleepy Hollow's waffle sandwiches get built on the base of a more standard textured waffle, allowing for folding — and for each nook and cranny to get filled with savory *and* sweet toppings.

For breakfast (and throughout the day), you can order the Fresh Fruit Waffle Sandwich, smothered in chocolate-hazelnut spread and then layered with fresh fruit like chopped strawberries, ripe blueberries, and fresh bananas. The combination of the fluffy, golden waffle; thick, creamy hazelnut spread; and bright fruit makes an unbeatable start to any Disney Parks day.

Craving a waffle for lunch? Head back to Sleepy Hollow for the Sweet-and-Spicy Chicken-Waffle Sandwich. With the same base waffle as the fresh-fruit version, this iteration takes a more savory route. The waffle gets topped with a generous portion of fried chicken breast thoroughly coated in a sticky, sweet, spicy sauce. As if the honey-sriracha glaze wasn't enough, it's then layered with broccoli slaw and served alongside house-made potato chips!

THE BEST CHURROS

Disneyland is more famous than Disney World for its churros, but the Anaheim resort doesn't corner the market on this crisp golden-brown treat. While you can find churros all around Disney World, there are two spots I always go to get the freshest, crispiest-yet-fluffiest churros on property.

First, head over to Nomad Lounge in Disney's Animal Kingdom, where they fry up churros fresh to order. Served with two dipping sauces, these churros are delicious, and they're a great twist on a theme-park favorite. Plus, as a bonus, they're gluten-free, so more people can enjoy them!

Heading out of the parks? Find the best churros at Walt Disney World at Capa, the award-winning, Spanish-style steakhouse at the Four Seasons Resort Orlando at Walt Disney World Resort. The Churros de Madrid are super authentic: With one sweet bite, you'll get transported from Florida to Spain. Served with a balanced chocolate sauce and a thick caramel dip, these churros are exactly as the dessert was intended to be — the perfect end to a Disney day. 🐭

LEFT: Walt Disney World's take on chicken and waffles elevates this popular ~~snack~~ *meal.* **PHOTO BY JUDD HELMS** | *ABOVE: Nomad Lounge's churros come with dipping sauces that make the flavors explode on your palate.* **PHOTO BY RAIN BLANKEN**

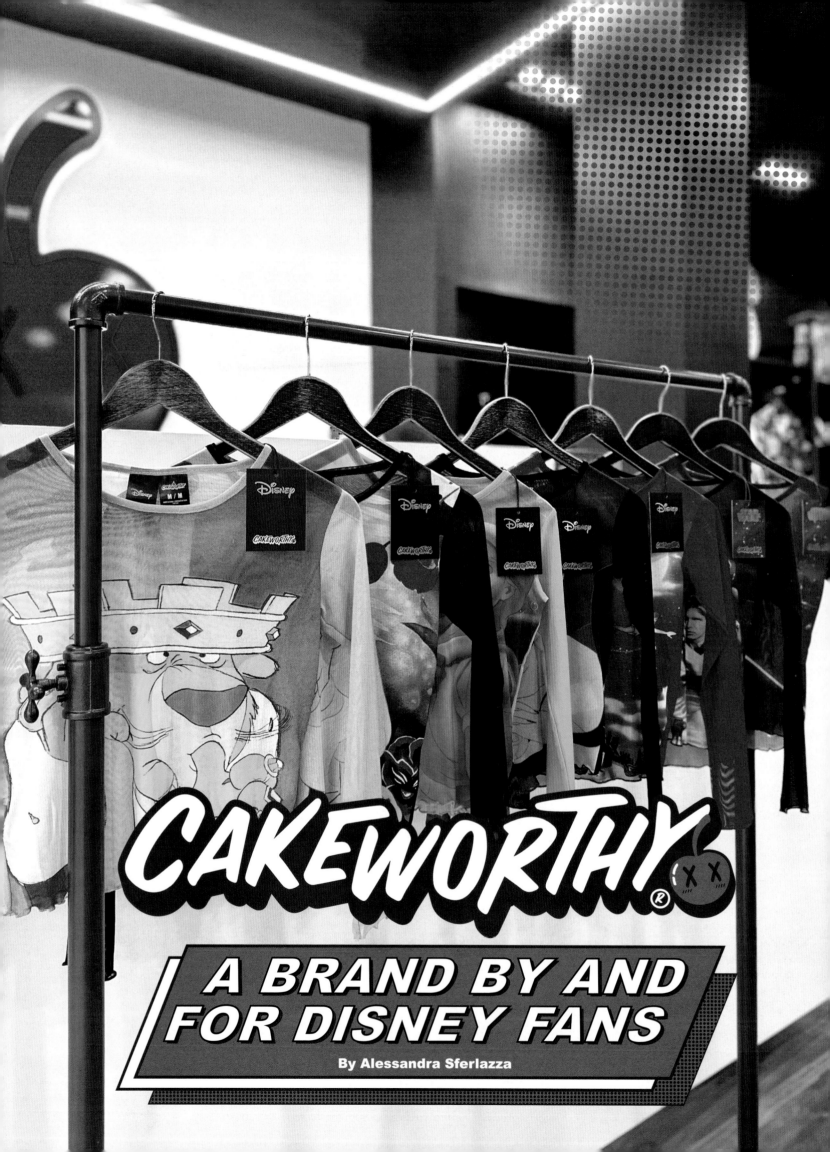

CAKEWORTHY.®

A BRAND BY AND FOR DISNEY FANS

By Alessandra Sferlazza

Cakeworthy is a Canadian-owned-and-operated brand fueled by fandoms. The fashion label began as an Etsy shop in 2014, when Brandon Sheddon, founder and CEO, screen-printed his own designs by hand in his home.

Cakeworthy has come a long way since then and is now carried by several online retailers, including shopDisney. The brand, which opened its first physical retail location a year ago, is well-known in the Disney community for its unique clothing licensed from Disney, Marvel, Lucasfilm, the Muppets, and Pixar.

Cakeworthy is a place for *all* fans. It's inclusive in its sizing and representation, offering size S through 4XL for most designs. Most of the clothes are also unisex.

WDW Magazine recently interviewed Brandon to learn how the brand has grown over the last decade — and what role fans have played.

Cakeworthy creator Brandon Sheddon at the retail opening in 2022. **PHOTO BY BARRY GRAY**

What inspired you to create a brand that celebrates a love of fashion and fandoms?

Honestly, it was a total accident. I was screen-printing some T-shirts in a spare bedroom and selling them on Etsy for fun. I had no intention of this ever growing anywhere near where it has today. It still blows my mind … I was creating pop culture-inspired shirts that were unisex for things that you couldn't really find in retail at that time. From there, we started getting a really cool fan base.

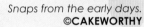

Snaps from the early days.
©CAKEWORTHY

I can't walk down Main Street, U.S.A. without seeing at least one of your signature all-over-print (AOP) shirts. How did it feel the first time you saw someone wearing one of your designs in a Disney Park?

I was in the elevator at Grand Floridian, and someone was wearing a T-shirt, and it was still like one of the ones that I was making in a spare bedroom. It said, "This chamber has no windows and no doors," just a plain white tee with a black print. And I remember looking at my partner and just being gobsmacked. And still, it's so cool! Anytime I go with friends, we are always like, "Oh, Cakeworthy! Oh, Cakeworthy!" And it's so cool.

The brand truly has something for every fan. ©CAKEWORTHY

PREVIOUS: From back-room business to big-time retail: Cakeworthy's retail location in Hamilton, Ontario. ©CAKEWORTHY

What are you most proud of your company for?

Standing out in such a competitive industry ... competing with other gigantic, well-known [brands] around the world; brands that are licensing like Coach or Vans. And obviously we're not at that level of popularity yet, so to be able to even just be in that same market is really cool.

This print is part of a new Disney100-themed collection
©CAKEWORTHY

What role have your fans played along your journey?

These flannels will fit any fan.
©CAKEWORTHY

We try to always listen to what our customers are telling us. We get so many DMs saying things like, "Oh, you should do something with this brand or that brand." Just something as simple as, "We wish your dresses had pockets." So now, some of our dresses have pockets.

The big advantage of being a smaller brand is that we have the ability to listen to our customers without having to jump through a million hoops.

What inspires an AOP, and how do you pick which elements to include in the final design?

We try to focus on the main characters, plus fan favorites. For example, I'll give you a sneak peek. We have a new *Hercules* AOP that just came out ... When you think of *Hercules*, it probably would traditionally have Hercules, Meg, Pegasus, and Hades. So instead of going in that direction, we did Hades and Pain and Panic, because I thought they had a really cool color scheme mixed together. It's very retro and bright.

The Pain and Panic AOP. **PHOTOS BY SARAH RUSSO**

For as long as I have been a fan, Cakeworthy was exclusively an e-commerce store. What made you decide to open the brick-and-mortar store in Hamilton, Ontario?

I feel like as a Canadian company, we really don't have a lot of local, grounded roots in Hamilton or even Ontario. I feel like we're well-known mostly in the U.S. ... But I really wanted an opportunity to connect with local fans and local customers and establish ourselves here ... When we had done our pop-ups and just [saw] people lining up at 5 in the morning in the rain to come check out some deals ... [it] was just really eye-opening. 🐭

WDW Magazine CEO Steph Shuster gets her Cakeworthy fix. **PHOTO BY DANNY SHUSTER**

This or That

Just because we all love Walt Disney World doesn't mean we don't have our favorites. We took to social media to ask our fans a series of *this or that* questions to find out what *your* top picks are.

Pirates of the Caribbean
OR
"it's a small world"

Mickey's Not-So-Scary Halloween Party
OR
Mickey's Very Merry Christmas Party

Classic Mickey
OR
Sorcerer Mickey

Early Morning Rope Drop
OR
Kiss Goodnight

PHOTOS BY WDW MAGAZINE PHOTOGRAPHY TEAM

DISNEYBOUNDERS
Favorite Bounds

BY LESLIE KAY

In 2021, we celebrated a decade of the DisneyBound community, and the years keep on coming! From DisneyBounding at home to DisneyBounding at Disney Parks, from Orlando and Anaheim to Shanghai and Tokyo, DisneyBounding has become a global phenomenon. And as *WDW Magazine* celebrates its decade milestone by focusing on fan favorites, we decided to ask our fans to show us their favorite DisneyBounds.

When I put out the call, I was not surprised to have my inbox flooded with hundreds of submissions. Not only were all the Bounds super-cute, but so many of them were accompanied by incredible stories about what made these Bounds so memorable. Fans shared stories of fun Disney Parks experiences, inspiring confidence boosts, touching moments with family and friends, and pure Disney magic!

It's through the DisneyBound community that so many (including myself) have found some of their best friends. That is *my* favorite part of the DisneyBounding experience. *What's yours?* 🐾

PHOTO BY @LIVINGWITHKATY

PHOTO BY @TAKEABREATHWITHALEXIS

PHOTO BY @WEARINGMAGIC

PHOTO BY @HELLOFAHEEMA

PHOTO BY @INTHEMIDDLEOFAFAIRYTALE

PHOTO BY @THENESSDIARIES_

 x **WDW** MAGAZINE

Want to see your bound in the magazine?
Keep an eye on @wdwmagazine and @thedisneybound for DisneyBound prompts, and show us your Disney style.

PARANORMAL THRILLS ON SUNSET BOULEVARD

THE MASTERFUL DESIGN OF THE HOLLYWOOD TOWER HOTEL

BY MATTHEW KRUL

At the end of Sunset Boulevard, a magnificent tragedy in another dimension awaits. **PHOTO BY CLIFF WANG**

Considered an Imagineering masterpiece, The Twilight Zone Tower of Terror opened at Disney's Hollywood Studios on July 22, 1994, and remains one of the most popular attractions at Walt Disney World. This paranormal attraction sends you into your own episode of *The Twilight Zone* as you board a maintenance service elevator in an abandoned hotel, enter the fifth dimension, and plummet 13 stories in a randomized sequence of drops.

While the ride system is what draws first-time visitors, the story-driven details are what entice fans to experience the attraction time and again. From beginning to end, Tower of Terror is designed to evoke a sense of uneasiness.

POSED FOR THE SPOTLIGHT

As the tallest structure in the park, Imagineers designed the Hollywood Tower Hotel to intrigue guests even from the opposite end of Sunset Boulevard. With its sharp corners, dreary colors, and charred appearance, the hotel seems cold

The "set dressing" around the building signals that this hotel had something bad happen… once upon a time. **PHOTOS BY ERNIE CARR**

The angled building allows for better photos. Scary selfie, anyone? **PHOTO BY CLIFF WANG**

and foreboding. Ironically, this ominous display contrasts a billboard behind The Trolley Car Café, which would otherwise seem to show vibrant, luxurious Hollywood accommodations. Imagineers intentionally created this juxtaposition to draw attention to the hotel's disrepair. It provides a clue that some kind of tragedy has befallen the hotel, transforming it from a beacon of light to a foreboding shadow of its former self.

Have you ever noticed how the Imagineers positioned the Hollywood Tower Hotel at an unusual angle? Rather than setting it perfectly perpendicular to the shops and cafes along Sunset Boulevard, they turned it about 45 degrees away from the street line. Imagineers designed it this way for photography, knowing that the angled profile of the Hollywood Tower Hotel would make for a great backdrop. It also allows you to see the depth of the building — the ride is longer than many might realize.

DISREPAIR AND DESPAIR

In the attraction queue, Imagineers wanted to build a sense of anxiety as you near

the entrance of the building, once again employing visual techniques. For instance, as you approach the lobby, you pass a dried-up pool surrounded by cracked concrete, decayed plaster, and overgrown vegetation. This indicates the resort hasn't been tended to in a long time. As you get closer to the door to the lobby, you then pass a plaque that reads "1917 A.D.," giving an idea of the age of this building and the tragic fate that has become of this once vibrant resort.

Imagineers really leaned into the state of disrepair inside the lobby. Covered in dust and cobwebs, the lobby's dim lighting and haunting fixtures evoke a sense of foreboding. Imagineers also left clues that some kind of disaster occurred, including old luggage that seems to have been left behind and a game of mahjong still unfinished. The musty and somewhat smoldering scent in the air combined with the haunting swing-era music echoing through the lobby create sensory anticipation as you approach the pre-show.

Inside the Twilight Zone Tower of Terror, Imagineers took great care to age and distress the lobby.

PHOTOS ON THIS PAGE BY CJ AYD, ERNIE CARR, AND CLIFF WANG

Here's the (however brief) view from the top. **PHOTO BY MIKE BILLICK**

Going up? Yes, but then down, down, and maybe up again. **PHOTO BY LAURIE SAPP**

RANDOMIZED SEQUENCING

In the original version of Tower of Terror, guests would experience one 13-story drop on the attraction (though original riders might remember a small "fake-out" drop before the full plummet). A few years later, Imagineers added a second drop to double the thrills. Eventually, Imagineers realized that they could create longer, randomized sequences for the ride, which would create an even greater sense of uneasiness, even for repeat guests.

One of my favorite stories about this updated version of the attraction has to do with one particular ride profile. Imagineer Theron Skees told me he would ride the attraction and frequently hear repeat guests telling their first-time companions exactly when the drop was going to happen. Wanting to create a surprise for these return visitors, he decided on a ride profile that would start by accelerating *upward* instead of downward. With this new sequence, even guests who have experienced the attraction hundreds of times still would have no idea whether they will first drop or rise on any particular day.

MASTERFUL STORYTELLING

To this day, Tower of Terror remains a masterclass of Imagineering. The building itself is still a thrilling addition to the park, but it's the carefully sequenced details and story that truly make this attraction an unforgettable experience. The next time you experience Tower of Terror, see if you can identify some of these intricate details on your way to the ride. 🐭

NOT SURE IF YOU WANT TO TAKE THE PLUNGE? CHECK IT OUT ON YOUTUBE.

ON THIS DAY IN DISNEY HISTORY...

OCT. 1 , 1988

Exactly 17 years after the opening of Walt Disney World, Disney's Caribbean Beach Resort opened to guests. The hotel was the first Moderate Resort at Disney World and, upon opening, was one of the largest hotels in Florida. The expansive property features five island villages where guests can stay: Aruba, Barbados, Jamaica, Martinique, and Trinidad. Today, the hotel is the hub for the Disney Skyliner.

OCT. 5, 2014

The day Maelstrom closed in the Norway Pavilion is one many EPCOT fans still lament. The boat ride opened on July 5, 1988, taking guests through scenes from Norwegian history. The ride closed permanently in 2014 to make way for the arrival of Frozen Ever After, which uses the same ride system to take guests through the story of *Frozen*.

OCT. 3, 1955

ABC began airing what would become one of the most popular children's TV series of all time: *Mickey Mouse Club*. When it first aired, the show lasted an hour, with episodes Monday through Friday. The talented kids of the program, or "Mouseketeers," performed musical numbers and various sketches. The original Mouseketeers included Annette Funicello and Cubby O'Brien.

OCT. 31, 1995

One of Disney World's most popular seasonal events began on Halloween 1995. The first Mickey's Not-So-Scary Halloween Party lasted one night only and cost $16.95 per person. Popularity for the party quickly grew; by 2001, the seasonal event spanned five nights. Now guests can visit select nights from August to early November.

Check out the full history archives on our blog.

BY CATHY SALUSTRI

On our first official date, I remember getting into Barry's car and hearing "No Sugar Tonight" playing on the CD player. So, while Guess Who didn't play the Garden Rocks Concert Series at EPCOT's International Flower & Garden Festival this past year, Ambrosia with Peter Beckett, the voice of Player, seemed like an excellent runner-up for a night devoted to only us.

In our day-to-day lives, Barry and I run a hyperlocal weekly newspaper together, I write for a variety of publications that don't *all* involve going to Disney World, and, when we went on an EPCOT date night this past April, I also had assumed a bevy of commitments. Once active people — we met working on a sailboat — most nights we now collapse, exhausted, on the couch.

But not this weekend. We'd escaped to Disney's Port Orleans Resort - Riverside with our trusty hounds, and, for four days, we had relatively few responsibilities.

Wherever you go, though, there you are, and that's why our "date night" actually started not with a romantic dinner in Italy but during the day, at a Behind the Seeds Tour of The Land. Barry and I long ago traded our turfgrass for a Florida landscape, planted some food-bearing plants and trees, and have a curiosity about how EPCOT manages to grow much of its own food.

Once at Behind the Seeds, we lagged behind as I took photos, dorked-out with everything (hi, Stanley!), and tried to

Go in-depth on the Behind the Seeds Tour in issue 113. Get your copy today.

WDW-MAGAZINE.COM/SHOP

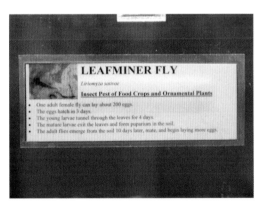

If these photos look like your idea of a perfect date night, Behind the Seeds may be the tour you and your loved one need to unwind. Not pictured: Stanley (IYKYK). **PHOTOS BY JUDD HELMS**

figure out where we could buy parasitoid wasps (I grow a lush crop of Everglades tomatoes at home, but they get leafminers every year). Then, because I am who I am, I asked if Walt Disney World uses GMOs (no, but they *do* use hybridization, a less-permanent gene-altering process used for centuries), and Barry asked, somewhat animatedly, why more countries couldn't use the methods Disney does (they can) because of how well those methods serve not only humanity, but the planet. In a flash, I realized we were the hippies in the group. Our guide answered every one of our questions knowledgeably and patiently, giving us plenty to talk about over dinner at Coral Reef.

At dinner, I realized I've *apparently* spent more time at Walt Disney World than I thought, because Jeff, our server, remembered me, the fact that I can't have gluten, and which dessert I liked the last time I ate there (the plant-based Baileys Almande and Jack Daniel's Mousse, with chocolate ganache and candied almonds).

We scored a table by the aquarium, so we divided our time between food, discussing the Behind the Seeds Tour, and watching the guitarfish who chilled on the seafloor by our window for pretty much our entire meal.

With every bite (and, in fact, every step at EPCOT), I enjoyed myself — and the idea we had nothing to do but spend time together — more and more. Freed from daily demands hammering at us, we talked about my career — and how many things I tend to say "yes" to doing even if, as Barry pointed out, I'm well past the point in my career where I need to say yes to everything.

PREVIOUS: Yes, it cost more than a dinner and movie, but Disney magic makes it more special, too. **PHOTO BY JUDD HELMS**

With time to spare — and seating to Garden Rocks guaranteed, thanks to a dining package — we strolled, hand in hand, past a multitude of countries. The colors and sounds of World Showcase streamed past, one blending with the next, as we took the time to step over to Command Performance, playing British Rock for other Gen X and Boomer fans — and one post-Gen-Z toddler who *really* loved The Who (although she'll never know the magic of Keith Moon).

A guaranteed spot gave us front-and-center seats to Ambrosia — and some time to spare before the show opened. In that time, we talked about realigning our lives, about how we could make more time for fun nights like these, and, most importantly, what we might have after the show for dessert.

We'd talked about ice cream cones on the BoardWalk, courtesy of Beaches & Cream, but when I booked the Garden Rocks dinner, I sort of overlooked that it came with an appetizer *and* dessert. Despite our post-dinner, pre-concert optimism, we couldn't cram anything else in our bellies, so the night ended with us back at Port Orleans - Riverside, with me

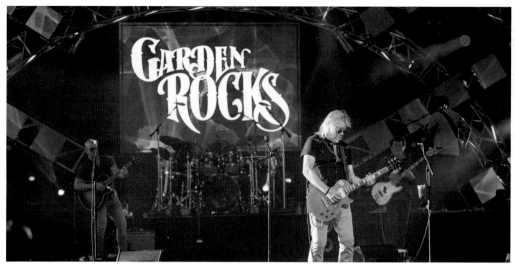

Peter Beckett, the Voice of Player, offered the perfect encore for our date night. **PHOTO BY CLIFF WANG**

trying to summon the energy to polish off the last of my shrimp and grits, the tiny, tasty remembrance of a day — and night — gone exceptionally well at EPCOT.

Looking back, what made the date special was that we made a decision to spend a day just for us. And, although, yes, it probably cost us more than a Lyft, drinks, and dinner back home, it wasn't the money spent that made it extraordinary. What made the day — and night — memorable was the time spent

reconnecting and talking about something larger than what we wanted for dinner or whether or not the dogs had their monthly heartworm chewable.

And that's the beauty of a date night at EPCOT (or, really, anywhere at Walt Disney World): It isn't something most of us do every week, so we set aside the minutiae of the day-to-day. In doing that, we leave room for the extra; the special moments that let us reconnect with who we are and who we love. 🐭

CHEERS!
A PLACE FOR WEARY WANDERERS: NOMAD LOUNGE

I f I could have one Walt Disney World eatery as my neighborhood watering hole, it would be Nomad Lounge. There's something special about this walk-up-only oasis at Disney's Animal Kingdom that makes it one of the best places in the world to dream of adventure. The décor, from the sink-into-them cocktail chairs to the polished wood bar with travel tag chandeliers hanging overhead, pays homage to the mystique of travel.

It's that spirit of travel that pushes me out of my comfort zone and into new, exciting territory. Whereas my taste buds usually gravitate toward lime and gin, I find myself ordering exotic cocktails that embody the spirit of Nomad Lounge — and, in fact, Animal Kingdom.

Today, my husband and I choose two: Nomad's version of a Mai Tai, the Lamu

Libation (Starr African Rum, Cruzan Banana Rum, and guava purée with orange, lime, and pineapple juices, topped with Gosling's 151 Rum) for me; the fruitier Leaping Lizard (Malibu Pineapple Rum and Leblon Cachaça with orange, passion fruit, and mango juices) for him.

We clink glasses, sip, and, for a moment, are on the tarmac on Casablanca, ready to fly off to parts unknown.

Cheers.

TEXT AND PHOTO BY CATHY SALUSTRI

ICE CREAM SANDWICH VS. PREMIUM BAR

AMBASSADOR SNACK SHOWDOWN

There is no Disney snack debate as divisive as the one between the Mickey's Premium Ice Cream Bar and Mickey's Premium Ice Cream Sandwich. And it extends all the way to Walt Disney World's Ambassadors.

"I'm a Mickey Premium Bar girl," Ambassador Ali Manion told us — and Raevon quickly jumped in with, "And I'm a Mickey Ice Cream Sandwich kind of guy."

They take their snacks quite seriously, but the rivalry is all in good fun. After all, no matter which you choose, you're still eating ice cream in the Most Magical Place on Earth!

Hooked on a Feeling
A Whole Universe to Remember

BY CATHY SALUSTRI

I n 1982, 9-year-old me rode Universe of Energy for the first time. I've since heard that people — kids, especially — thought the ride was too long and boring, but not me. I loved everything about this opening-day EPCOT attraction, from the magnetic-powered cars that felt as big as a theater to the *eau de swamp* smell.

The giant attraction — each ride vehicle held 97 people — had a two-acre footprint. I've never been what you could call "tall" in the conventional sense, and I was even less so at 9 years old, so it makes sense that my earliest overwhelming impression of Universe of Energy was that it, well, *overwhelmed* me.

SPIRIT IN THE SKY

Today, I can look around my neighborhood and see a few roofs dotted with solar panels (and one of my neighbors has a business selling integrated solar panels), but in 1982, solar panels were akin to *Jetsons*-esque technology like flying cars and computers you could fit in your hand. The Universe of Energy, despite an Exxon sponsorship, boasted 2,200 solar panels on its roof, and although those solar panels only provided about 15% of the attraction's power needs, today we can see it foreshadowed The Walt Disney Company's philosophy about responsible environmental stewardship.

Planet protection aside, lots of the features inside the Universe of Energy made guests *marvel*. After all, this was Future World — and this attraction offered plenty of new tech for guests. The first new bit of technology revealed itself in the pre-show, which, instead of playing on a flat screen, happened on something called a kinetic mosaic. Created by Emil Radock, a Czechoslovakian filmmaker, the mosaic consisted of 100 separate pieces, each one three-sided, with one black side and two white sides. Five projectors cast the pre-show onto these pieces, giving a kaleidoscope effect as guests learned about different types of energy. The pre-show film showcased everything from fossil fuels to mechanical energy to nuclear energy, leaning heavily into the first law of thermodynamics (no one can create or destroy energy, but energy can change forms).

After the pre-show, guests boarded those massive ride vehicles where — wait for it —

they saw *another* film, this time projected on a traditional screen (making the animated film, projected on the 155-foot-wide screen, the largest projection of an animated movie, anywhere). This animated film taught people about how fossil fuels formed, which made for a logical segue into the ride part of the attraction: Primeval World. The slow-moving vehicle followed a guide-wire track — invisible to guests, so it seemed as if the cars moved by some sort of magic. In reality, the guide wires used radio signals to move the vehicles.

Another film played at the end of the ride, alluding to the future of energy. This film displayed traditionally, except for the mirrors that amplified the effect of the film. Using the conceit of a radio broadcast, Imagineers took guests into the future of energy — which was decidedly non-fossilized. Remember, Universe of Energy opened not quite five years after the 1979 gas crisis that had people waiting in line for gas for hours at a time. Alternatives to fossil fuels seemed prudent, even to a pint-sized me, who vividly remembers waiting in those gas lines in the passenger seat of an un-air-conditioned car.

GO ALL THE WAY

Between the pre-show and the ride itself, Universe of Energy lasted up to 62 minutes. That included 17 minutes of pre-show, although guests could enter the pre-show at any point. Cast Members discouraged people from sitting on the floor during the pre-show, issuing repeated but polite refrains on the microphone. No worries for tired legs, though: The seated part of the attraction lasted a whopping 45 minutes, making it the longest ride on property.

Universe of Energy entrance circa 1988. **PHOTO RESTORATION BY BILL COTTER**

NEXT PAGE TOP: Universe of Energy entrance sponsored by Exxon, circa 1982. **PHOTO RESTORATION BY BILL COTTER** | *MIDDLE: Universe of Energy, as it appeared during the Ellen era.* **PHOTO BY BRETT SVENSON** | **BOTTOM:** *Cosmic Rewind now brings a different sort of universe — and energy — to this storied building.* **PHOTO BY CLIFF WANG**

The original Universe of Energy has given way… **PHOTO BY CLIFF WANG**

…to a whole new universe. Or should we say, multiverse? **PHOTO BY CLIFF WANG**

I WANT YOU BACK

Around the time *Jurassic Park* hit theaters, the dinosaurs — previously presented in muted, dignified colors — took on some new flashes of color. I didn't mind the flourishes these new upstarts boasted, but I did mourn the 1996 closure of my beloved attraction (OK, so it didn't *really* belong to me, but I did ride it *a lot*.) *Why*, I whined, *does Disney have to change things we love?*

I'M NOT IN LOVE

Once I actually experienced Ellen's Energy Adventure, I stopped whining, because Ellen DeGeneres and Bill Nye were, of course, the shot in the arm this attraction needed. Ellen represented all of us (the guests) who knew almost nothing about energy, and Bill Nye — well, he's the Science Guy; what else do you need to know about why he made the perfect energy sherpa?

Along for the ride — metaphorically, at least — were Alex Trebek, Tim Conway, and Jamie Lee Curtis. Ellen's Energy Adventure (originally Ellen's Energy Crisis, but only for a blip) started in Ellen's NYC apartment (where no one ever locks their doors!) and morphed into a dream sequence where she competed on *Jeopardy!*, facing off against her college-era frenemy Judy and Albert Einstein. To help her learn about energy — because she's no match for her old "friend" — Bill Nye led her back in time to those same dinosaurs we saw in the original attraction (with a few minor changes).

Ellen and Bill Nye the Science Guy took me back in time for the last time in

2017. I keenly remember thinking the Imagineers knew nothing about what Disney fans loved — why else would they mothball this perfect attraction?

FEEL THE FLOW

While I'll never really stop loving Universe of Energy and Ellen's Energy Adventure, *Guardians of the Galaxy*: Cosmic Rewind reminds us, subtly, that the Universe of Energy — like energy itself — never really goes away. Nevertheless, the attraction has almost completely disappeared from EPCOT.

Almost.

When you board Cosmic Rewind, you'll find subtle nods to its predecessor. You can read them all online on our blog, but I'll let you in on my favorite: Keep a keen ear peeled when you ride the coaster, and you'll hear the rock version the Universe of Energy theme song.

It's nice to have a bit of both.

WONDERING ABOUT THOSE EASTER EGGS? CHECK OUT THE FULL LIST ON OUR WEBSITE.

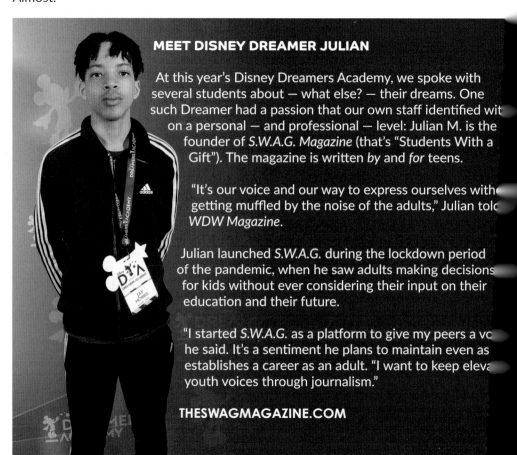

MEET DISNEY DREAMER JULIAN

At this year's Disney Dreamers Academy, we spoke with several students about — what else? — their dreams. One such Dreamer had a passion that our own staff identified wit on a personal — and professional — level: Julian M. is the founder of *S.W.A.G. Magazine* (that's "Students With a Gift"). The magazine is written *by* and *for* teens.

"It's our voice and our way to express ourselves with getting muffled by the noise of the adults," Julian told *WDW Magazine*.

Julian launched *S.W.A.G.* during the lockdown period of the pandemic, when he saw adults making decisions for kids without ever considering their input on their education and their future.

"I started *S.W.A.G.* as a platform to give my peers a vc he said. It's a sentiment he plans to maintain even as establishes a career as an adult. "I want to keep eleva youth voices through journalism."

THESWAGMAGAZINE.COM

This or That

Just because we all love Walt Disney World doesn't mean we don't have our favorites. We took to social media to ask our fans a series of *this or that* questions to find out what *your* top picks are.

**EPCOT International
Food & Wine Festival
OR
Flower & Garden Festival**

**Orange Bird
OR
Figment**

**Starting World
Showcase from Mexico
OR
Canada**

**Collecting pins
OR
Ears**

DID YOU KNOW ?

FAN FAVORITES AT WALT DISNEY WORLD

BY TIMOTHY MOORE